D0825086

STUDY GUIDE for
African Americans in the U.S. Economy

STUDY GUIDE for
African Americans in the U.S. Economy

CECILIA A. CONRAD

JOHN WHITEHEAD

PATRICK MASON

JAMES STEWART

with Michael Enriquez
and Claudia Sitgraves

ROWMAN & LITTLEFIELD PUBLISHERS, INC.
Lanham • Boulder • New York • Toronto • Oxford

ROWMAN & LITTLEFIELD PUBLISHERS, INC.

Published in the United States of America
by Rowman & Littlefield Publishers, Inc.
A wholly owned subsidiary of The Rowman & Littlefield Publishing Group, Inc.
4501 Forbes Boulevard, Suite 200, Lanham, MD 20706
www.rowmanlittlefield.com

P.O. Box 317, Oxford OX2 9RU, UK

Copyright © 2005 by Rowman & Littlefield Publishers, Inc.

All rights reserved. No part of this publication may be reproduced, stored in a retrieval
system, or transmitted in any form or by any means, electronic, mechanical, photocopying,
recording, or otherwise, without the prior permission of the publisher.

British Library Cataloguing in Publication Information Available

Library of Congress Cataloging-in-Publication Data Available

ISBN 0-7425-4379-X (pbk. : alk. paper)

Printed in the United States of America

♾™ The paper used in this publication meets the minimum requirements of American
National Standard for Information Sciences—Permanence of Paper for Printed Library
Materials, ANSI/NISO Z39.48-1992.

Contents

Preface

THIS STUDY GUIDE is designed to help you read and understand the text, *African Americans in the U.S. Economy*. It contains a chapter for each of the forty-three chapters of the text. Each *Study Guide* chapter contains the following pedagogical features:

1. **Key Terms and Institutions**. You should be able to define the terms and identify the institutions after reading the chapter.
2. **Key Names**. Most chapters include a list of important people. You should be able to identify these people and describe their achievements or contributions.
3. **True/False Questions**. These questions should help you quickly grasp the main ideas of each chapter.
4. **Multiple-Choice Questions**. Deepen your understanding of the readings by choosing the best answer from four alternatives. Examine all the alternatives to be sure you can distinguish why your choice is the best.
5. **Essay Questions**. Sharpen your analysis by using the reading to support your own ideas. These questions were designed to point out main ideas and often to build on previous material. Answering the questions completely should improve your critical thinking skills.

In addition, each of the book's nine sections will be summarized in the *Study Guide*. Section summaries are designed to tie the material in each section together so that you can see the logical progression of the ideas presented.

How to Use the *Study Guide*

Before you read a chapter in the text, read the chapter abstract/summary and look over the key terms and institutions in your *Study Guide*. As you read the text, refer often to the institutions, relationships, and terms outlined in the *Study Guide*. If you encounter a number of unfamiliar terms or concepts, you need to reread the text.

Only when you feel comfortable with the material outlined in the *Study Guide* are you ready to tackle the true/false and multiple-choice questions. Many of the study guide chapters contain true/false and multiple-choice questions (exercises) that are ranked according to level of difficulty with the most difficult questions at the end of the exercise. If you find any of these questions extremely difficult, do not attempt to guess the correct answer—reread the text. Although many of these questions are quite rigorous, they should be within your grasp. You should pay close attention to details.

Following the true/false and multiple-choice questions are essay questions. Many students skip these questions because their instructors emphasize objective questions on examinations. This is a mistake. These exercises tie concepts together. By working the essay questions, you will comprehend the relationships among concepts and institutions in the chapter and will better understand the material.

As a final suggestion, you will increase the usefulness of this *Study Guide* if you combine it with an important resource—your fellow students. For example, you might consider forming a study group with other students to compare your answers to the questions in the *Study Guide*. Your study group should make a list of the questions you answered incorrectly and review the concepts covered by these questions. This will help you prepare for exams.

The *Study Guide* may not reduce the amount of time that you devote to your class, but when used properly, it can help you study more effectively.

Acknowledgments

We would like to thank David Burns, Helen Bechan, Danielle Herring, Pan Phu Phu, and Alfa Yansane for their contributions to the development of this study guide. We are also grateful for the support that the Social Sciences Department at City College of San Francisco and the Department of Economics at Pomona College gave us in preparing this study guide.

I

Slavery and the Early Formation of Black Labor

THE CHAPTERS IN PART I chronicle how systematic exploitation of Africans, and later African Americans, fueled nineteenth-century economic growth in western industrial economies. The Atlantic slave trade and its role in spurring economic activity in Europe and in various parts of the Western Hemisphere are the first topics addressed in the section. The rise and expansion of plantation agriculture and the consolidation of chattel slavery provided the critical foundations for slave-based agriculture to serve as the bedrock for pre–Civil War economic growth in the United States. Various aspects of this exploitative economic system are described in several of the chapters. Other issues explored in this section include the treatment of blacks under slavery—including physical and mental coercion, denial of rights, and basic human needs, the fate of blacks who remained tied to southern agriculture after the Civil War, and the entry of African Americans into the northern industrial labor force. Overall, the chapters provide solid documentation of the important historical role played by blacks in building the U.S. economy and important evidence in support of the contemporary reparations movement. Direct links between historical oppression and contemporary inequalities are suggested in several chapters.

Philip S. Foner's chapter, "The International Slave Trade," describes the origins of the international slave trade and its role in financing the British industrial revolution. Foner argues that Britain dominated other European nations involved in the trade as slavery evolved into a purely economic venture. William A. Darity Jr.'s chapter, "Africa, Europe, and the Origins of Uneven Development: The Role of Slavery," explores many of the same issues, but he also links the wealth created by the slave trade to the contemporary prosperity of the United States and Europe. Darity contrasts the health of Western economies to stagnation in many African countries and attributes this phenomenon to the devastating effects of the slave trade on Africa. In the next chapter, "The Critical Role of African Americans in the Development of the Pre–Civil War U.S. Economy," James B. Stewart focuses specific attention on how black labor was mobilized on plantations to generate profits that fueled southern and national economic growth. He also describes the conditions facing blacks at the end of the slavery regime that laid the foundation for current racial economic inequality.

The last two chapters in this section provide accounts of the economic circumstances of African Americans following the Civil War. Daniel Fusfeld and Timothy Bates's chapter, "The Black Sharecropping System and Its Decline," focuses specific attention on the fate of black agricultural workers following the Civil War. The operation of the sharecropping system is described with particular attention paid to how farmers were kept in perpetual debt. Factors leading to the decline of sharecropping are explained, including the eroding importance of cotton to the agricultural economy and the introduction of machines that replaced agricultural workers. In the last chapter, "The Rise of the Black Industrial Working Class, 1915–1918," Philip S. Foner examines how World War I created new employment opportunities for blacks in the urban North, spurring a large-scale emigration of blacks from the South. Foner also describes how the decline in these employment opportunities after World War I did not prevent blacks from establishing a permanent presence in the industrial working class, nor did it stem the rising tide of migration from the South to the North.

5. How do the main views of this chapter support contemporary claims for black reparations?

Additional Essay Questions

6. What economic and ideological factors played a major role in the start and development of colonial slavery and the Atlantic slave trade? Explain your answer.
7. Describe and explain the impact of slavery on Africa and her people.

NAME

CHAPTER

3

The Critical Role of African Americans in the Development of the Pre–Civil War U.S. Economy

James B. Stewart

Key Terms and Institutions

Atlantic slave trade
Black artisans
Chesapeake Region
Civil War
Colonial economic development
Cotton gin
Distribution of slave ownership
Exoduster movement
Gang labor system
House servants
Human capital

Human capital accumulation
Intellectual property rights of slaves
International slave trade
Marginal product
Opportunity cost
Overseers
Per-Capita Income of Slave South
Task labor system
Tufts University Center on Hunger
    and Poverty
Transcontinental trade

Key Names

Ronald Bailey
Henry Blair
John Blassingame
Stephen Crawford
William A. Darity Jr.
W. E. B. DuBois
Stanley Engerman
Robert Fogel
E. Franklin Frazier
Lowell Galloway
Eugene Genovese
Lorenzo Green
Herbert Gutman
Cheryl Harris
Janet Herman
Joseph Inikori

David Klingman
James Marketti
Karl Marx
Patrick Mason
Benjamin Montgomery
Isiah Montgomery
Larry Neal
John Olsen
Robert Ransom
Joe Trotter
Mark Smith
Kenneth Stamp
Richard Sutch
Richard Vedder
Gavin Wright

Note: The true/false and multiple-choice questions below are ranked according to level of difficulty. For example, true/false questions # 1 and 2 below are less difficult than questions # 9 and 10.

True/False Questions

Indicate whether each of the following statements is True or False by placing a "T" for true or an "F" for false in the space provided.

_____ 1. On the eve of the American Revolution, most African slaves in the North American colonies were engaged in sugar cultivation.

_____ 2. Between 1820 and 1830, cotton production in the South increased by about 700,000 bales.

_____ 3. The major labor systems under which enslaved Africans performed agricultural work involved strict supervision by overseers.

_____ 4. Throughout the antebellum South, enslaved Africans faced more favorable and less difficult working conditions under the task system than under the gang labor system.

_____ 5. The view that it was nearly impossible for slaves to develop stable family relationships is supported by recent research cited in this chapter.

_____ 6. In the1850s, Southern industries that used slave labor were generally more profitable than similar industries employing free labor.

_____ 7. Stewart's analysis suggests that a very large percentage of the white population in the antebellum South benefited from slavery.

_____ 8. Enslaved blacks were not permitted to work in skilled occupations.

_____ 9. Robert Fogel's work supports claims that the diet provided to slaves had a major impact on black educational (human capital) advancement.

_____ 10. The percentage share of agricultural output going to black sharecroppers and tenant farmers was larger than the percentage share going to their black slave counterparts.

_____ 11. In the post–Civil War period, black inventors continued to lack intellectual property rights over their inventions.

_____ 12. The profits generated from the slave trade were nearly as important as the growth of the New England textile industry in directly advancing the industrial revolution in the United States.

_____ 13. The distribution of slave ownership was highly skewed.

_____ 14. Prior to the invention of the cotton gin, tobacco production was central to each North American colony.

_____ 15. From 1800 to 1860, the legal status of the Atlantic slave trade in the United States supported the increased demand for black labor to produce cotton.

_____ 16. By 1860, individual white slave owners in the South owned, on average, approximately two slaves.

_____ 17. In the period immediately following the Civil War, the slave owners in general experienced a significant decline in their ability to exploit black labor.

_____ 18. While most enslaved Africans who were transported across the Atlantic went to Brazil, only a relatively small percentage of them went to the colonies that eventually became the United States.

_____ 19. Between 1820 and 1860, cotton production in the U.S. South increased by about 400 percent.

_____ 20. The increased demand for black labor in the Southern economy resulting from the invention of the cotton gin led to an increase in the importation of enslaved Africans.

_____ 21. It can be inferred from the chapter that per-capita income in the antebellum South was higher than in the North.

_____ 22. There is general consensus among economic historians that slavery was a highly efficient system.

_____ 23. The chapter cites evidence that, between 1850 and 1870, the real income of slave owners using the gang labor system increased by 70 percent.

_____ 24. In 1820, enslaved blacks received a larger percentage of the value of their contribution to total output than the percentage they received in 1850.

_____ 25. An approximate average number of slaves owned by white families in the South cannot be determined by the information provided in the chapter.

Multiple-Choice Questions

Circle the letter that corresponds to the (one) best answer.

1. Recent research cited in this chapter supports the view that:
   a. it was impossible for slaves to maintain a stable family system.
   b. there is no link between plantation size and and the chances for enslaved blacks to develop stable family relationships.
   c. enslaved blacks found it easier to develop stable family relationships on large plantations than on small plantations.
   d. none of the above.

2. The gang labor system:
   a. involved strict supervision by overseers.
   b. was relatively efficient.
   c. generally yielded less than normal profits.
   d. a and b above.

3. In the post–Civil War period, the literacy rate among artisans was _____ times higher than among farm laborers.
   a. two
   b. three
   c. four
   d. five

4. A major weakness of estimates of the present value of losses incurred by blacks as a result of slavery is that they fail to take into account losses resulting from:
   a. barriers on black educational advancement.
   b. restrictions on the ability of enslaved blacks to develop mutual aid networks.
   c. restrictions on the ability of enslaved blacks to develop stable family relationships.
   d. none of the above.

5. Gavin Wright's work suggests that:
   a. plantation slavery in the South was both efficient and profitable.
   b. the high per-capita income growth rates in the antebellum South were the result of the efficiency of the gang labor system.
   c. the high per-capita income growth rates in the antebellum South were the result of the rapid growth of world demand for cotton.
   d. b and c.

6. Which of the following is not true?
   a. About 25 percent of the total income in Southern states was the result of slave exploitation.
   b. Estimates of the present value of losses (measured in 1983 dollars) incurred by Africans resulting from their enslavement over the 1720–1860 period range from $2.1 to 4.7 billion.
   c. In the two decades prior to the Civil War, about 15 percent of the total assets in the United States were generated from slave labor.
   d. By some estimates, total wealth accumulated from slavery by the onset of the Civil War was about 3.2 million in 1859 dollars.

7. In the post–Civil War period, opportunities for blacks to acquire human capital:
   a. greatly increased.
   b. actually decreased.
   c. remained at a low level.
   d. became a major goal of Southern industrialists.

8. Slave owners attempted to achieve optimal levels of output primarily through:
   a. the threat of the "whip."
   b. using the task labor system on an extensive basis.
   c. forcing their slaves to work a relatively high number of hours per year.
   d. coercing artificially high levels of output per hour.

9. In 1860, about _____ percent of of the slaves in the South lived in urban areas.
   a. 1.75
   b. 2.75
   c. 3.5
   d. 4.5

10. Stewart's analysis implies that slave owners were able to raise the productivity of slave labor (i.e., output per unit of slave labor) by:
    a. increasing the capital/labor ratio.
    b. increasing the labor/capital ratio.
    c. decreasing the capital/labor ratio.
    d. none of the above.

11. Between 1820 and 1830, cotton production increased by about _____ percent.
    a. 100
    b. 133.3
    c. 233.3
    d. none of the above

12. From the information provided in the chapter, which of the following statements is probably true?
    a. In 1860, most of the slave-owning families owned nine or more slaves.
    b. In 1860, the top 12 percent (on the income scale) of the slave-owning families in the South owned, on average, about forty-two slaves.
    c. An approximate average number of slaves owned by families in the South in 1860 cannot be determined by the information provided in the chapter.
    d. None of the above are true.

13. If we assume that 15 percent of the slaves in the antebellum South were not engaged in cotton production, then in 1860 the output per unit of slave labor (working in cotton production) was about _____ .
    a. 85 percent.
    b. 1.32 bales of cotton.
    c. 7.5 bales of cotton.
    d. 15 bales of cotton.

Essay Questions

1. Describe and explain the various strategies used by slave owners to achieve desired levels of agricultural output.

2. Discuss the impact of the invention of the cotton gin on slavery in the United States.

3. Describe and explain the contributions of slavery and the Atlantic slave trade to the growth of the textile industry in New England between 1790 and 1860.

4. List and describe at least three losses/costs blacks incurred as a result of slavery.

5. In what ways did whites economically gain from slavery? Cite specific evidence from the chapter to support your answer.

Additional Essay Questions

6. Summarize and discuss the arguments and evidence that support the view that slavery was both efficient and highly profitable.
7. James B. Stewart points out that black labor was exploited outside of plantation agriculture. What was the contribution of nonagricultural slave labor to pre–Civil War economic growth in the United States?
8. Discuss the distribution of slave ownership among white southern families in 1860.
9. Do you agree or disagree with the view that white gains from slavery were transferred intergenerationally and are currently enjoyed by whites? Explain your position.
10. How does the chapter help you understand contemporary black reparations claims?

CHAPTER

4

The Black Sharecropping System and Its Decline

Daniel Fusfeld and Timothy Bates

Key Terms and Institutions

Agricultural adjustment program
Cash tenants
Debt peonage
Sharecroppers

Sharecropping
Share tenants
Wage laborers

Note: The true/false and multiple-choice questions below are ranked according to level of difficulty. For example, true/false questions # 1 and 2 below are less difficult than questions # 9 and 10.

True/False Questions

Indicate whether each of the following statements is True or False by placing a "T" for true or an "F" for false in the space provided.

_____ 1. The majority of tenant farmers worked on large plantations.

_____ 2. White tenant farmers outnumbered black tenant farmers.

_____ 3. Share tenants faced the possibility of losing their equipment if the crop they produced was not enough to pay off debt at harvesttime.

_____ 4. Cash tenants were the most common type of black agricultural workers.

_____ 5. Sharecroppers faced higher prices for food and other necessities because purchases were restricted to particular stores and commissaries.

_____ 6. State legislation helped to perpetuate the sharecropping system.

_____ 7. The Agricultural Adjustment Program (AAA) was designed to assist former sharecroppers who transitioned to industrial work.

_____ 8. As mechanization increased in the cotton belt, the number of sharecroppers rose.

_____ 9. The white landowners' rationale for the black sharecropping system was very similar to their rationale for plantation slavery.

_____ 10. Government programs in the 1930s failed to increase farm incomes for landowners.

_____ 11. Sharecroppers paid a 10 percent effective rate of interest for food and other necessities purchased on credit from landlords.

_____ 12. The chapter implies that share tenants and croppers exercised relatively little or no autonomy over the conditions of their work on the larger plantations.

_____ 13. The chapter suggests that after debt peonage was declared illegal by the Supreme Court in 1911, most share tenants were able to escape their indebtedness status.

_____ 14. Sharecroppers were less financially affluent than cash tenants and share tenants but were economically better off than wage laborers.

_____ 15. During the 1930s, over 60 percent of agricultural workers pushed out of southern tenant status were black.

Multiple-Choice Questions

Circle the letter that corresponds to the (one) best answer.

1. Cash tenants:
   a. received their equipment from the landowner and paid as rent about 1/2 of their cotton crop.
   b. owned some of their own equipment and paid as rent between 1/4 and 1/3 of their cotton crop.
   c. owned their own equipment, paid cash as rent, and made their own decisions about growing and marketing crops.
   d. were employed by the day when they were needed but were not guaranteed any fixed amount of work.

2. Share tenants:
   a. received their equipment from the landowner and paid as rent about 1/2 of their cotton crop.
   b. owned some of their equipment and paid as rent between 1/4 and 1/3 of their cotton crop.
   c. owned their equipment and paid cash as rent, making their own decisions about growing and marketing crops.
   d. were employed by the day when they were needed but were not guaranteed any fixed amount of work.

3. Sharecroppers:
   a. received their equipment from the landowner and paid as rent about 1/2 of their cotton crop.
   b. owned some of their equipment and paid as rent, between 1/4 and 1/3 of their cotton crop.
   c. owned their equipment and paid cash as rent, making their own decisions about growing and marketing crops.
   d. were employed by the day when they were needed but were not guaranteed any fixed amount of work.

4. Wage laborers:
   a. received their equipment from the landowner and paid as rent about 1/2 of their cotton crop.
   b. owned some of their equipment and paid as rent between 1/4 and 1/3 of their cotton crop.
   c. owned their equipment and paid cash as rent.
   d. were employed by the day when they were needed but were not guaranteed any fixed amount of work.

5. Major components of the diet of tenant families included all of the following *except*:
   a. salt pork.
   b. cornmeal.
   c. potatoes.
   d. molasses.

6. All of the following are true about the mobility of tenants *except*:
   a. tenants in debt could not relocate until the debt was paid.
   b. tenants not in debt could change landlords as frequently as desired.
   c. tenants were generally restricted from leaving the land until after harvesttime.
   d. in many cases fleeing the community was the only realistic escape from tenancy arrangements.

7. U.S. cotton producers began losing world market share in the 1920s to all of the following countries *except*:
   a. Egypt.
   b. India.
   c. Brazil.
   d. Canada.

8. All of the following factors contributed to reduced demand for black tenant agricultural workers *except*:
   a. a decrease in world demand for U.S. cotton.
   b. increased mechanization of cotton farming.
   c. the Great Depression.
   d. all of the above were factors contributing to reduced demand for black tenant workers.

9. Landowners used all of the following strategies to limit AAA benefit payments to tenants *except*:
   a. increasing the number of tenants to increase production and their portion of payments.

   b. applying tenants' payments to satisfy outstanding debts.
   c. changing tenants' status to that of wage laborer.
   d. mechanization of farming methods.
10. Between 1920 and 1924, the number of cotton bales ginned in Green County, Georgia, decreased by about _____ percent.
   a. 52.5
   b. 68.1
   c. 75.6
   d. 213

Essay Questions

1. Describe the four types of Southern agricultural workers who did not own land.

2. Explain why sharecroppers were likely to be in a constant state of debt.

3. Describe the barriers that sharecroppers faced in escaping their status.

4. Describe the living conditions for share tenants and croppers.

5. What was the attitude of white landowners toward tenants?

6. Explain the shifts in the sharecropping system that occurred in the 1920s and 1930s.

Additional Essay Questions

7. What effect did the government's AAA have on black farmers and their families?
8. Explain the stages of the mechanization of cotton farming between the 1930s and 1950s and its impact on black agricultural workers.
9. How did the sharecropping system and government agricultural programs contribute to unequal wealth accumulation between blacks and whites?

CHAPTER

5

The Rise of the Black Industrial Working Class, 1915–1918

Philip S. Foner

Key Terms and Institutions

Atlanta Agreement
The Chicago Defender
Colored Branch of the New York State
    Employment Bureau
Division of Negro Economics

Great migration
Ku Klux Klan (KKK)
National Urban League
Southern landowners
Trade unions

Key Name

Henry Ford

True/False Questions

Indicate whether each of the following statements is True or False by placing a "T" for true or an "F" for false in the space provided.

_____ 1. Prior to World War I, blacks were largely excluded from jobs in the North *except* for domestic and personal services.

_____ 2. The number of black industrial workers nearly doubled from 1910 to 1920.

_____ 3. The great migration North of blacks was primarily caused by economic factors.

_____ 4. Southern landowners supported the migration of blacks by offering transportation subsidies.

_____ 5. The demand for black labor in the South slackened considerably in the months following World War I.

_____ 6. Black servicemen returning from World War I faced high rates of unemployment.

_____ 7. The migration of blacks to Northern industrial cities declined between 1922 to 1924.

_____ 8. Many blacks left Northern industrial areas after World War I due to the rise in demand for their labor in the South.

_____ 9. In 1921, the black unemployment rate in Detroit was roughly three times higher than the rate for whites in this city.

_____ 10. Trade unions discouraged apprenticeships, leading to a decline in the number of black artisans during the 1910s.

_____ 11. Overall, black workers made significant economic advances between World War I and the mid-1920s.

Multiple-Choice Questions

Circle the letter that corresponds to the (one) best answer.

1. All of the choices below were reasons why blacks migrated to the North during 1915–1918 _except_ for:
   a. segregation in the South.
   b. war production caused an increase demand for labor.
   c. passage of restrictive immigration laws.
   d. the military draft caused a labor shortage.

2. The great migration North of blacks during World War I was primarily due to:
   a. Jim Crow segregation in the South.
   b. the lack of black access to educational facilities in the South.
   c. the absence of black political rights in the South.
   d. war-related demand for black labor in the North.

3. Which of the following statements is _incorrect_?
   a. Between emancipation and World War I, blacks held a significant number of skilled occupations in the North.
   b. The boll weevil contributed to the decline of Southern agriculture.
   c. In 1920, one-third of all gainfully employed blacks were working in American industry.
   d. The demand for black labor in the North slackened in the months after World War I.

4. Shortly after 1916, Southern landowners:
   a. sold large plots of land to foreign industrialists.
   b. sold large plots of land to foreign banks.
   c. supported Ku Klux Klan efforts to exterminate the black population in the South.
   d. supported state and local legislation to stop the migration North of blacks.

5. When World War I ended, most blacks:
   a. returned to the South.
   b. were retrained for skilled jobs in the peacetime economy.
   c. were recruited to join white unions.
   d. lost their jobs to white workers returning from the war.
6. The late Henry Ford:
   a. allowed a significant number of blacks in his plants to hold high level managerial jobs.
   b. allowed a small number of blacks in his plants to hold skilled occupations.
   c. employed a relatively large number of foreign immigrants.
   d. none of the above.
7. The reason most blacks remained in unskilled industrial positions during World War I was that:
   a. employers and unions made agreements to keep blacks out of skilled positions.
   b. there was a surplus of skilled white workers who had more experience.
   c. the demand for skilled labor decreased during the war.
   d. all of the above.
8. A second migration of blacks to the North occurred because:
   a. Southern landowners passed laws restricting the activities of Northern recruiters.
   b. restrictive immigration laws reduced competition for jobs.
   c. trade unions increased apprentice opportunities for blacks.
   d. the government banned discrimination in hiring for skilled jobs.
9. As a result of the Atlanta Agreement:
   a. black workers received equal wages to white workers for performing the same job.
   b. black workers were fired from all jobs in the railroad industry.
   c. many black workers retained the positions they had held previously.
   d. many black workers were forced from their previous positions into menial jobs.
10. The number of black artisans declined as a result of:
    a. white industrialists discouraging black participation in apprenticeship programs.
    b. trade unions discouraging black participation in apprenticeship programs.
    c. blacks moving into automotive and shipbuilding occupations.
    d. none of the above.

Essay Questions

1. Describe the factors that led to the great migration of blacks during World War I.

2. How did Southern landowners respond to the great migration?

3. Describe the demand for black labor in the North after World War I.

4. Describe the ways that trade unions, employers, and the government discriminated against black workers.

Additional Essay Questions

5. Discuss the overall impact of World War I on black economic well-being.
6. Do you feel that the migration of blacks to the Northern industries was generally an economic advance? Why or why not? Cite specific evidence from the chapter to support your position.

Organized Labor and African Americans

PART II CONTINUES the examination of black labor in the post–Civil War period. The chapter by William Harris, "An Uncertain Tradition: Blacks and Unions, 1865–1925," chronicles both early attempts to recruit black workers into organized labor and racist union practices that excluded most blacks from most trade unions in the period immediately following the Civil War. This exclusion from white unions led to the formation of independent black labor unions, including the Brotherhood of Sleeping Car Porters. Philip S. Foner's chapter, "The Brotherhood of Sleeping Car Porters," extends Harris's story by discussing the brotherhood's early history, from the election of A. Phillip Randolph as its first president, to its effort to secure higher wages and better working conditions for Pullman Company workers, to its official affiliation in 1929 with the American Federation of Labor (AFL). Both chapters highlight conflicts within the black community over whether to support unionization or cooperation with white employers as the best strategy to advance black economic well-being.

James B. Stewart's chapter, "Civil Rights and Organized Labor: The Case of the United Steelworkers of America, 1948–1970," provides a detailed case study of the treatment of civil rights issues within organized labor. He examines the history of race relations and civil rights enforcement within the United Steel Workers of America (USWA) from 1948 to 1970. His chapter reveals that although USWA introduced bureaucratic structures to address civil rights issues, the impact of these structures was minimal because of bureaucratic inertia and the lack of a solid commitment from USWA's white leadership. Stewart concludes with praise for two of the labor movements more recent activities: the American Federation of Labor-Congress of Industrial Organizations' (AFL-CIO's) attempts to establish alliances with African American ministers, and the AFL-CIO's Economic Education Project, which was designed to reverse prevailing political fragmentation among workers.

NAME

CHAPTER

6

An Uncertain Tradition: Blacks and Unions, 1865–1925

William Harris

Key Terms and Institutions

American Federation of Labor (AFL)
Brotherhood of Locomotive Firemen
Brotherhood of Sleeping Car Porters
Division of Negro Economics
Knights of Labor
The Messenger

National Association for the
   Advancement of Colored People
   (NAACP)
The Niagara movement
Pullman Company
Pullman Palace Car Company
U.S. Department of Labor

Key Names

Eugene V. Debs
Frederick Douglass
W. E. B. DuBois
T. Thomas Fortune
Samuel Gompers

Dr. George Edmund Haynes
T. Arnold Hill
Kelly Miller
George M. Pullman
Booker T. Washington

True/False Questions

Indicate whether each of the following statements is True or False by placing a "T" for true or an "F" for false in the space provided.

_____   1. Blacks were excluded from membership in the major railroad unions.

_____   2. In its early years, the AFL was without a clearly defined position toward black workers.

_____   3. The AFL convention of 1900 gave official sanction to segregated locals for blacks.

_____   4. Booker T. Washington and his followers encouraged blacks to line up with organized labor during periods of industrial strife.

_____   5. Higher wages became the most important grievance of black porters during the 1920s.

_____   6. A small number of blacks became managers in the Pullman Company.

_____   7. Many blacks participated in the great railroad strike of 1894.

_____   8. Booker T. Washington supported a positive relationship between black labor and white capital while giving qualified support to organized labor with intent of countering white attitudes. (Hint: remember an essay includes all elements, including the references, footnotes, and notes/endnotes).

_____   9. The Niagara movement promoted the view that, because of the racism of white workers, the interests of black workers and organized labor were in general conflict.

_____   10. According to Harris, the implementation of "federal" unions for black workers would have represented a crucial step toward advancing the economic well-being of this group of workers.

_____   11. During the 1890s, the national leadership of the AFL supported black labor entry into the rank-and-file membership of the AFL.

_____   12. During World War I, leaders of the NAACP and the National Urban League (NUL) supported increased black-white labor solidarity.

_____   13. Black professionals were very critical of black strike-breakers.

_____   14. The NUL was founded in 1911 to promote black entrepreneurship in Northern urban communities.

_____   15. W. E. B. DuBois succeeded Eugene V. Debs as leader of the radical Niagara movement.

_____   16. The chapter implies that, in the early years of the NAACP, many of its members supported a positive relationship between blacks and the captains of industry.

_____   17. It can be inferred from the essay that, despite their early views on the extent to which blacks should align with labor versus capital, the NUL became more prolabor than the NAACP in the period immediately following 1919.

_____   18. During the late 1880s, blacks constituted at least 13 percent of the Knights of Labor membership.

_____ 19. The base pay of porters in 1926 would have had to increase by 158 percent to equal the income needed for the average urban family to maintain an adequate standard of living.

Multiple-Choice Questions

Circle the letter that corresponds to the (one) best answer.

1. The NAACP convention of 1919:
   a. marked the first time the NAACP took a position against organized labor.
   b. marked the first time the NAACP discussed labor problems in convention.
   c. marked the first time the NAACP came out in support of segregated black unions.
   d. called on black leaders to break down antiunion views among black workers.
2. The great railroad strike of 1894:
   a. led to improved working conditions for black porters.
   b. marked the beginning of a new era of labor-management relations within the Pullman Company.
   c. marked the beginning of black participation in the organized labor movement.
   d. represented an instance of working-class racial solidarity.
3. The Pullman Company's response to labor organizing resulted in:
   a. more members of the Brotherhood of Sleeping Car Porters (BSCP) over time.
   b. overwhelming white support of blacks' union organizing activities.
   c. many black sleeping car porters losing their livelihood.
   d. none of the above.
4. Which of the following was _not_ a factor that led George M. Pullman to hire only black men as porters?
   a. George Pullman's concern for the welfare of blacks.
   b. The fact that it was a mark of status among whites to be waited on by blacks.
   c. The fact that blacks were a cheap source of labor.
   d. The social distance between blacks and whites.
5. The chapter suggests that white locals prevented black entry into the craft trades through:
   a. charging blacks excessively high membership dues.
   b. charging blacks excessively high union dues.
   c. restricting black entry into apprenticeship programs.
   d. all of the above.
6. Kelly Miller, a prominent civil rights activist during the 1920s, supported:
   a. a strong alliance between blacks and organized labor.
   b. the concept of independent black unions.
   c. a strong alliance between blacks and their capitalist employers.
   d. none of the above.

7. The Knights of Labor:
   a. sought to organize blacks to further the interest of white workers.
   b. actively promoted working class racial solidarity.
   c. officially excluded blacks from its membership.
   d. a and b above.
8. After 1896, Samuel Gompers:
   a. underwent an evolution in his attitude toward blacks and their participation in organized labor.
   b. supported organizing blacks into the AFL.
   c. supported AFL policies that would lead to results unfavorable to blacks.
   d. none of the above.
9. During the 1920s, A. Phillip Randolph frequently took the position that the Pullman Company only hired black men as porters:
   a. because a mark of status among whites was to be served by blacks.
   b. because the company wanted to maintain the defining power relationship that prevailed between blacks and their plantation masters during the antebellum South.
   c. because hiring white men as porters would have insulted class conscious white customers who wanted the lowest paying, personal service jobs to be distributed among blacks.
   d. as a result of its interest in advancing the general welfare of blacks.
10. T. Arnold Hill, the first director of the National Urban League's (NUL's) new Department of Industrial Relations in 1925, argued that:
    a. the individual competition among blacks and whites was not responsible for racism in America.
    b. individual racism is far less important than institutional racism.
    c. white capitalists were responsible for the low economic status of blacks.
    d. all of the above.
11. In general, local unions in the early history of organized labor:
    a. instituted policies that promoted the development of black craftsmen.
    b. followed the line of their national leaders regarding racial membership policies.
    c. shared their national leaderships' beliefs in the need for labor solidarity among white and black workers.
    d. none of the above.
12. All of the following directly or indirectly resulted from the migration of blacks into Northern urban areas, between 1910 and World War I, *except*:
    a. increased interest in black-white labor relations among black leaders and northern white unionists.
    b. creation of the NUL.
    c. creation of the NAACP.
    d. creation of a special division within the U.S. Department of Labor responsible for providing the Secretary of Labor with information on the status of black workers.

13. William Harris's essay suggests that:
    a. Booker T. Washington's views carried dominant influence upon the ideological direction of early twentieth-century black thought.
    b. Booker T. Washington's views carried broad influence upon the ideological direction of early twentieth-century black thought.
    c. W. E. B. DuBois's views carried heavy influence upon the ideological direction of early twentieth-century black thought.
    d. Washington's and DuBois's views carried about equal weight over the ideological direction of early twentieth-century black thought.

Essay Questions

1. Discuss the factors that prevented black entry into organized labor during the 1920s.

2. Discuss the conditions facing black porters during the 1920s.

3. Explain why many blacks became strike-breakers during major industrial strikes in the early 1900s.

4. Describe the activities and accomplishments of the National Urban League during its early years.

Additional Essay Questions

5. Describe T. Arnold Hill's position on black-white labor solidarity.
6. Describe and trace the evolution of Samuel Gompers's position toward black workers and their participation in organized labor.
7. Summarize and evaluate Kelly Miller's position regarding blacks and trade unionism in 1925.

CHAPTER

7

The Brotherhood of Sleeping Car Porters

Philip S. Foner

Key Terms and Institutions

Brotherhood of Sleeping Car Porters
Company union
Employee Representation Plan
Hotel and Restaurant Employees
 International
The Messenger

Pullman Company
Pullman Porters
The Railroad Mediation Board
The Railroad Mediation Act
Welfare workers

Key Names

E. F. Casey
John Fitzpatrick
A. Phillip Randolph

Ashley L. Totten
Milton P. Webster

True/False Questions

Indicate whether each of the following statements is True or False by placing a "T" for true or an "F" for false in the space provided.

_____   1. The Employee Representation Plan (ERP) was basically a company union.
_____   2. Ashley L. Totten is credited with introducing A. Phillip Randolph to the cause of the black porters.
_____   3. By 1926, only a quarter of the porters supported the Brotherhood.
_____   4. Milton P. Webster was the first vice president of the Brotherhood of Sleeping Car Porters.
_____   5. The Hotel and Restaurant Employees' International union, which claimed jurisdiction over the Brotherhood, had a provision in its constitution that established the inferior status of black workers.
_____   6. Initially, the majority of Chicago's black leaders supported the formation of the Brotherhood of Sleeping Car Porters.
_____   7. William Green, while president of the AFL, supported the Brotherhood because of its anti-Communist leadership.
_____   8. In 1928, the Interstate Commerce Commission ruled that tips were not an adequate substitute for wages.
_____   9. *The Messenger* became a voice through which black porters could openly express their grievances.
_____   10. The black press generally supported the early efforts of the Brotherhood.
_____   11. The majority of black porters favored collective bargaining.
_____   12. Most of the AFL Internationals were against giving the brotherhood an international charter on the grounds that such action would threaten the existence of segregated unions.

Multiple-Choice Questions

Circle the letter that corresponds to the (one) best answer.

1. Which tactic did the Pullman Company use to discourage union organizing efforts?
   a. Firing workers who were involved in organizing.
   b. Subsidies to the black press.
   c. Physical attacks on union organizers.
   d. All of the above.
2. Which of the following was used by black leaders to undermine the efforts of the Brotherhood?
   a. Relatively high wages of black porters.
   b. The long record of the Pullman Company hiring blacks.
   c. Pullman's Employee Representation Plan.
   d. None of the above.

3. Randolph finally agreed to affiliate the Brotherhood of Sleeping Car Porters with:
   a. the Hotel and Restaurant Employees' International.
   b. the AFL as "federal unions" of the federation.
   c. the AFL International.
   d. the Employee Representation Plan.
4. Many black workers came to see the formation of the Brotherhood as a:
   a. test of the ability of black workers to build and maintain an effective union.
   b. threat to cooperative relations between black workers and white capitalist employers.
   c. major vehicle for black-white labor solidarity.
   d. threat to the well-being of black workers.
5. All of the choices below were reasons why the Brotherhood of Sleeping Car Porters was organized *except*:
   a. low wages and long hours.
   b. porters were required to remain on call without pay.
   c. lack of adequate rest on trips.
   d. porters wanted to start a retirement fund.
6. The porters' demands drafted on August 25, 1925, included:
   a. an elected representative to the Employee Representation Plan.
   b. an increase in wages and the end of tipping.
   c. the creation of a porter assistant position to help with job duties.
   d. all of the above.
7. The Employee Representation Plan was:
   a. established by the Pullman Company to discourage union consciousness.
   b. primarily established to address the grievances of black porters.
   c. responsible for the porters receiving a substantial increase in pay.
   d. all of the above.
8. The Brotherhood became an underground organization below the Mason-Dixon line to:
   a. avoid harassment from racist Southern unionists.
   b. avoid violent confrontations with thugs hired by the Pullman Company.
   c. avoid harassment by the Ku Klux Klan.
   d. protect the anonymity of its leadership in the South.
9. In calling off the porter's strike, Randolph was most influenced by:
   a. the company's readiness to hire replacement workers.
   b. a lack of support for the strike in the black press.
   c. William Green's advice to launch an education campaign about workers' grievances.
   d. the Railroad Mediation Board's decision that a strike was not justified.
10. A debate between A. Phillip Randolph and Perry Howard led to:
    a. the quick and sudden demise of the Employee Representation Plan.
    b. a significant number of porters becoming members of the Brotherhood.
    c. broad porter support for the Employee Representation Plan.
    d. black leaders giving unconditional support to the Brotherhood.

Essay Questions

1. What was the attitude of black porters toward unionism?

2. Describe the working conditions that convinced many porters that they needed a union.

3. Explain why the ERP was viewed as a company union.

4. Discuss the purpose of the Brotherhood's threatened strike against the Pullman Company. Describe the impact of this threatened strike.

5. Describe the victories and setbacks during the organizing of the Brotherhood of Sleeping Car Porters, including how the Pullman Company responded to the activities of the Brotherhood.

Additional Essay Questions

6. Describe the relationship that existed between black leadership and the Brotherhood. Was the relationship positive or negative? Explain.
7. Describe A. Phillip Randolph's attitude toward the AFL.
8. What is the significance of the Brotherhood in the history of the U.S. labor movement?

CHAPTER

8

Civil Rights and Organized Labor: The Case of the United Steelworkers of America, 1948–1970

James B. Stewart

Key Terms and Institutions

Affirmative action

AFL unions

Black Power movement

CIO unions

Civil Rights Act of 1964

Civil rights movement

Committee to Abolish Racial
    Discrimination

Congress on Racial Equality

Equal Employment Opportunity
    Commission (EEOC)

Fair Employment Practices Campaigns

NAACP Legal Defense Fund

Newport News Agreement

Revolutionary Union movement

Seniority

United Steelworkers of America

USWA Civil Rights Committee/
    Department

Wagner Act

Key Names

Melvyn Dubofsky

Michael Goldfield

Nelson Lichtenstein

Thomas Shane

Emmett Till

Willard Wirtz

True/False Questions

Indicate whether each of the following statements is True or False by placing a "T" for true or an "F" for false in the space provided.

_____ 1. The USWA was largely unwilling to modify its seniority procedures to address concerns of minority union members.

_____ 2. The author points out that internal union measures on civil rights issues were often impeded by sluggish bureaucracy.

_____ 3. In April of 1970 the central USWA staff was about 18 percent black.

_____ 4. The chapter implies that unions were helpful in reducing the discrimination of employers but attempted to maintain their internal white power structure.

_____ 5. The Director of the Civil Rights Department of the USWA found that most discrimination claims were related to seniority.

_____ 6. Stewart argues that political fragmentation among union workers has diminished the political power of organized labor.

_____ 7. The Secretary of Labor showed indifference to the grievances of black steel and shipyard workers.

_____ 8. Bethlehem Steel's summer jobs program for youth was lauded by the USWA as a method for minorities to gain vital experience.

_____ 9. It is argued in the chapter that to remain relevant, future unions will need to allow more flexibility for their workers.

_____ 10. USWA measures for addressing racial inequities in workplaces were more effective than what blacks could do using measures external to the union.

_____ 11. Progress on racial equality was difficult to verify for the USWA Civil Rights Committee because it remained detached from black workers.

_____ 12. The USWA leadership was about as diverse as that of its membership.

_____ 13. Research by Michael Goldfield reveals that the AFL unions became less racially egalitarian over time.

_____ 14. Unions were generally in agreement with the tenets of the civil rights movement.

_____ 15. Collective bargaining power of unions and individual rights are shown to have worked in tandem to improve conditions of employment for minorities.

_____ 16. USWA inaction in response to the lynching of Emmett Till showed a disregard for the rights of blacks.

Multiple-Choice Questions

Circle the letter that corresponds to the (one) best answer.

1. The Ad-Hoc Committee of black steelworkers advocated a three-point program, including each of the following changes *except*:
   a. reorganizing the Civil Rights Department.
   b. raising employment of blacks in district and national union offices.
   c. reducing the racial bias in seniority practices.
   d. increasing black membership on the Executive Board.

2. The Fair Employment Practices Campaigns were described as unsuccessful for all of the following reasons *except*:
   a. inability to achieve consensus among racial groups.
   b. lack of adequate funding.
   c. dearth of qualified people for leadership positions.
   d. weak organization.
3. Passage of the Civil Rights Act of 1964 created a _____ between the labor movement and the civil rights movement.
   a. link
   b. synergy
   c. quarrel
   d. wedge
4. The author's viewpoint on the future usefulness of unions can be described as:
   a. doubtful due to their weakening over recent decades.
   b. hostile since unions impede free market outcomes.
   c. confident that they will take the steps deemed necessary.
   d. hopeful that they will become inclusive and gain political power.
5. The "black caucus" formed to redress all of the following issues *except*:
   a. improved handling of civil rights complaints.
   b. unequal pay schemes.
   c. appointment of a nonblack to a subdistrict directorship.
   d. inadequate numbers of blacks in USWA leadership slots.
6. The results of the 1950 mail survey revealed all of the following *except*:
   a. that Northern locals were strongly overrepresented in the responses.
   b. that many responses did not acknowledge discrimination in locals that are likely to have had some.
   c. that minorities who complained of union bias were treated unfavorably.
   d. that several responses used the dearth of minority workers as evidence that there must not be much discrimination.
7. It can be inferred from the chapter that the Wagner Act:
   a. did little to advance the cause of civil rights.
   b. created tensions between union workers of different ethnicities.
   c. established the right of individual workers to remain nonmembers of unions.
   d. was effectively weakened by the successes of the civil rights movement.
8. Stewart argues that problems encountered by the USWA could have been avoided if:
   a. the union leadership had strongly supported civil rights measures.
   b. workers had exhibited more patience regarding social changes.
   c. society had been more understanding of the biases faced by minorities.
   d. government policy provided harsher penalties for racial discrimination.
9. USWA actions regarding racial equality can be described as:
   a. lacking in scope and effort.
   b. institutional advances that lagged worker expectations.
   c. dismissive of evidence on discrimination.
   d. eager to improve the conditions for minority employment.

Essay Questions

1. Summarize how the external efforts of the USWA differed from internal efforts regarding racial equality.

2. Explain why groups such as the USWA Civil Rights Committee/Department and the Congress on Racial Equality were formed.

3. Explain Stewart's point of view regarding the historical events described in the chapter and what they imply for future action.

4. Discuss the actions taken by government entities such as the EEOC and Labor Department in regards to the USWA. What can federal politics of the time reveal about their positions?

Additional Essay Questions

5. What does the chapter reveal about regional differences regarding race relations over 1948–1970? Explain.
6. Given the inequalities that existed in and prior to 1948–1970, why might the USWA have had difficulty finding leadership that was concerned about civil rights progress? Explain.
7. Using knowledge about the demographic shifts that have occurred since 1970, discuss what this chapter leads you to believe about post–1970 union cohesion and power. Is your response in line with what actually happened?

Theories of Racial Discrimination, Inequality, and Economic Progress

THE CHAPTERS IN PART III summarize and critique various theories that attempt to explain the persistence of racial economic discrimination and inequality. The first chapter in this section discusses several variants of the two major economic discrimination models within conventional economic analysis, generally categorized as "conservative" and "liberal." None of the discrimination models within these two paradigms pass the double test of logical consistency and empirical plausibility. Most of the theoretical models presented in this section have been influenced by or developed within radical racial economic discourse. Many radical critiques of racism were developed in the post–World War II period in response to the major flaws in the racial research generated by conventional economic analysis. Analyses of the strengths and weaknesses of early radical critiques provide the building blocks for most of the chapters in this section.

John Whitehead's chapter, "Racial Economic Inequality and Discrimination: The Conservative and Liberal Paradigms Revisited," challenges the adequacy of conservative and liberal racial economic analysis as useful paradigms to explain the persistence of racial economic inequality. Conservative racial analysis explains black-white economic inequality as primarily the result of blacks making poor individual choices and not the result of racial discrimination. In contrast, liberal racial analysis links black-white economic disparities to past virulent forms of racism, structural changes in the economy, and other broad social forces that are beyond the control of the individual. Whitehead's essay suggests that, while liberal racial analysis is informed by a less formal set of assumptions and concepts than conservative analysis, both theories have several weaknesses and fail the test of empirical plausibility. Whitehead concludes that neither conservatives nor liberals have developed an adequate theoretical model of how capitalism can exploit a racial distribution of resources. Peter Bohmer's chapter continues Whitehead's discussion of the capitalism-racism nexus by looking at its treatment within the Marxist theory of racism and racial inequality. Bohmer argues that a major strength of Marxist theory is its conceptualization that capitalism is an exploitative system that reaps significant economic benefits from a racially divided working class. However, his analysis also shows that the Marxist solution to racial exploitation—namely, an inter-racial and unified working class—is not without major problems.

The chapter by Timothy Bates and Daniel Fusfeld, "The Crowding Hypothesis," presents a radical version of the crowding model. While the paper is essentially written in the Marxist tradition, Bates and Fusfeld use conventional supply and demand theory as applied to labor markets to argue that the crowding of black workers into the secondary (low wage) job sector accounts for black-white income differentials and other racial economic outcomes. Mary C. King's chapter, " 'Keeping People in Their Place': The Economics of Racial Violence," goes beyond the reach of the other chapters by linking the concept of racial violence to the analysis of racial economic disparities. Her essay suggests that one way to understand the impact of racial violence on economic outcomes is to see it as enforcing unwritten property rights in "whiteness." Her chapter also shows that much of the racial economic progress in the civil rights era was the direct result of the riot years of the late 1960s.

James B. Stewart and Major Coleman's chapter, "The Black Political Economy Paradigm and the Dynamics of Racial Economic Inequality," examines the economic implications of race and racialized behavior with special attention to the linkages between "racial identity production" and economic disparities. Stewart and Coleman conceptualize racial identity production as a kind of individual and group property that can produce both income and wealth generation. In addition, collective identity is seen as having economic value and, therefore, the conclusion is drawn that groups will give up income and wealth to protect identity production. Stewart and Coleman's interpretations of the reasons for racialized behavior and the persistence of racial economic inequality differ markedly from other explanations in this section.

3. Summarize and explain Thomas Sowell's position on discrimination and government intervention.

4. Describe Lester Thurow's statistical discrimination model. Do you agree or disagree with his model? Explain.

5. Summarize and explain the major weaknesses of liberal racial analysis.

6. Summarize Wilson's position on the changing significance of race and class.

7. Describe and explain the position of Wilson and other liberal structuralists regarding race-specific policies. Do you agree or disagree with the liberal structuralist position? Explain.

Additional Essay Questions

8. Describe and evaluate Thomas Sowell's views regarding the civil rights movement.
9. Summarize and explain Gunnar Myrdal's "cumulative process" model.
10. Describe the impact of economic restructuring on black economic well-being.
11. Summarize the author's criticism of Wilson's race/class position. Do you agree or disagree with the author's criticism? Explain.

CHAPTER

10

Marxist Theory of Racism and Racial Inequality

Peter Bohmer

Key Terms and Institutions

Class reductionism
Economic determinism
Exploitation
Jim Crow
Monopoly capitalist class

Plessy v. Ferguson
Reserve Army of Unemployed Workers
Segmented labor markets
Superexploitation
White supremacy

Key Names

Gary Becker
Milton Friedman

Karl Marx
Michael Reich

Note: The true/false and multiple-choice questions below are ranked according to level of difficulty. For example, true/false questions # 1 and 2 below are less difficult than questions # 9 and 10.

CHAPTER

"Keeping People in Their Place": The Economics of Racial Violence

Mary C. King

Key Terms and Institutions

Antimiscegenation laws
American Indian Movement
Treaty of Guadalupe Hidalgo

War on Drugs
"zoot-suit race riots"

Key Names

Derrick Bell
Cheryl Harris

Rodney King

Note: The true/false and multiple-choice questions below are ranked according to level of difficulty. For example, true/false questions # 1 and 2 below are less difficult than questions # 9 and 10.

True/False Questions

Indicate whether each of the following statements is True or False by placing a "T" for true or an "F" for false in the space provided.

_____ 1. The Texas Rangers are described as a baseball team that gives opportunities to minority youth.

_____ 2. Research cited in the paper shows that a state supreme court struck down a murder conviction of a white man because the witnesses were Korean.

_____ 3. It is estimated that the native population in the United States and Canada declined by more than 90 percent.

_____ 4. A large majority of the race riots over the years 1954 to 1992 took place in the period of 1966 to 1968.

_____ 5. Racial income disparity is greater among women than it is among men.

_____ 6. The chapter suggests that there is an inverse relationship between racial riots and black-white income inequality.

_____ 7. Research cited in the chapter claims that African American children had worse growth conditions than those in Vietnam or Cambodia.

_____ 8. The author claims that police brutality is largely accepted.

_____ 9. King states that most lynchings of African Americans were motivated by suspicion of a black man's sexual interest in a white woman.

_____ 10. Outbreaks of violence against Asian Americans typically occurred during tough economic times.

_____ 11. Evidence shown in the paper reveals that the incomes of black women have risen steadily relative to white women since 1954.

_____ 12. King is highly critical of all forms of racial violence.

Multiple-Choice Questions

Circle the letter that corresponds to the (one) best answer:

1. Institutions listed in the chapter as doing violence to minorities include all of the following *except* those that:
   a. exploit low-skilled labor.
   b. give inferior education.
   c. cause inadequate medical care.
   d. maintain high poverty rates.
2. The kind of interracial violence focused on in this chapter is:
   a. illegal.
   b. illegal but generally ignored by government authorities.
   c. legal.
   d. all of the above.
3. To say that the race riots of the late 1960s challenged property rights in whiteness is to say that:

   a. violence served to push whites toward less discriminatory practices toward blacks.

   b. rioters violently challenged white property owners.

   c. rioters took the assets of white property owners by violence.

   d. television coverage of the riots increased the impact of the riots.

4. Which of the following corresponded with the greatest improvement in the racial income ratio over 1965–1988?

   a. For men, a riot occurring last year.

   b. For women, a riot occurring two years ago.

   c. For women, no riot incident.

   d. For men, a riot occurring this year.

5. The concept of property in whiteness means:

   a. that you had to be white to own property during much of U.S. history.

   b. that being white served as an economic asset, providing access to the best education, jobs, business opportunities, etc.

   c. that only nonwhites could be bought and sold as property.

   d. that whiteness is a metaphysical, not material, quality.

6. A strong criticism of King's ideas would be that:

   a. race riots were also perpetrated by minorities.

   b. the United States, despite its history, now provides lots of equality.

   c. Asian Americans have higher incomes than whites.

   d. other nations treat ethnic minorities in even worse ways.

Essay Questions

1. In your own words, what does it mean to say that people have had "property" in whiteness? How does property in whiteness relate to ownership of other forms of property?

2. How has the legal standing of people of color historically played into their vulnerability to violence?

3. How does the author argue that the race riots of the late 1960s affected black economic standing? What other explanations are possible for the pattern of black economic progress?

4. How can you apply the idea that violence is used to protect property rights to an issue other than race? For instance, how has violence been used to maintain economic privileges for men, or for heterosexual people?

Additional Essay Question

5. This chapter has described violence as a collective, or group, strategy to maintain property in whiteness, or to challenge them. Can you think of other group strategies people have employed, either historically or currently, to maintain or challenge economic benefits for whites? What about individual strategies?

CHAPTER

13

The Black Political Economy Paradigm and the Dynamics of Racial Economic Inequality

James B. Stewart and Major Coleman

Key Terms and Institutions

Collective-action mechanism
Collective racial identities
Cultural identity production
Cultural production conflicts
Cultural production externalities
Cultural production process
Economic coercion
Endogenous
Exogenous
Externalities (negative and positive)
Individual decision making
Neoclassical economists
"No Child Left Behind"
Phenotypic characteristics
Prison Industrial Complex

Property in whiteness
Public bads
Public goods
Quasi-artificial enterprise
Racial classifications
Racial identity
Racially segregated suburban conclaves
Racial stratification
Residential segregation
Social disequilibrium
Spatial mismatch
Stratification economics
Suburbanization of jobs
Taste for discrimination
White privilege

Key Names

Kenneth Arrow

Gary Becker

Albert Breton

W. E. B. DuBois

John Kain

True/False Questions

Indicate whether each of the following statements is True or False by placing a "T" for true or an "F" for false in the space provided.

_____ 1. In the black political economy (BPE) paradigm, individual choice is the only determinant of how racial identity influences economic outcomes

_____ 2. Neoclassical economics generally treats social identities such as racial identity as economically productive attributes.

_____ 3. In the context of the BPE paradigm, rural communities accept the presence of prisons with high proportions of black inmates in part because the status difference limits negative effects on white cultural identity production.

_____ 4. The BPE and neoclassical models agree that it is not possible for discrimination to persist in the long run because it can only be maintained at a prohibitive cost to those practicing discrimination.

_____ 5. The BPE paradigm rejects the interpretation that civil rights laws were intended to eliminate economic disparities between blacks and whites.

_____ 6. According to the BPE paradigm interracial conflicts are totally unrelated to the production and reproduction of collective racial identities.

_____ 7. Members of racial/ethnic minority groups who actively identify with majority group members can gain unrestricted access to "property rights in whiteness" and "white privilege."

_____ 8. It is not possible for members of one group to benefit from the cultural production of another group.

_____ 9. Blacks and whites are likely to engage in the same type of political activities in efforts to reduce the negative effects of each others' racial identity production.

_____ 10. In the BPE paradigm the rules and procedures associated with public policies are influenced significantly by the relative political and economic power of competing interest groups.

_____ 11. The work environment can be structured to minimize the effects of cultural production conflicts on income-generating activities.

_____ 12. Friendship between members of different racial/cultural groups is always independent of differences in racial identity production.

_____ 13. In the BPE paradigm, belonging to a racial group is a form of affiliation similar to voluntary membership in an organization.

_____ 14. One of the major underlying tensions in the workplace is the disruption of the traditional status hierarchy of positions with whites in higher status occupations and blacks in lower level jobs.

_____ 15. From the vantage point of the BPE paradigm one reason that immigrants have fewer barriers to obtaining employment than blacks is because their cultural identity production of immigrants generates fewer negative externalities for whites.

_____ 16. Becker's "taste for discrimination" model suggests that owners of capital who discriminate by race will eventually be driven out of a competitive industry.

_____ 17. In the BPE model, racial discrimination and other racialized behaviors are endogenously given.

_____ 18. The BPE paradigm suggests that the negative aspects of interracial contact can be eliminated through clear incentives for cooperative intergroup behavior.

_____ 19. Without government intervention or some other collective-action mechanism, "public goods" would likely be underproduced.

_____ 20. In the BPE model, there are strong economic incentives for black-white working class cooperation and unity.

_____ 21. The BPE paradigm does not support the view that racial economic outcomes can be significantly reduced by more blacks responding appropriately to existing market opportunities.

_____ 22. In the BPE paradigm, race is purely and simply a function of class stratification.

_____ 23. The BPE paradigm suggests that racial stratification resulting in the disproportionate assignment of high status positions to whites is an integral feature of the U.S. social formation.

_____ 24. The chapter suggests that, while African Americans in general are more negatively affected by the "suburbanization of jobs" than whites, low-income whites and low-income minorities are more or less equally affected by this phenomena.

_____ 25. From the standpoint of the BPE paradigm, racial groups will, as a general rule, prefer to give up income, but not wealth, to protect identity production.

Multiple-Choice Questions

Circle the letter that corresponds to the (one) best answer.

1. In the BPE paradigm, all of the following are characteristics of racial identity _except_:
    a. it is a form of individual property.
    b. it is a form of group property.
    c. it can contribute to income and wealth generation.
    d. all are characteristics of racial identity in the BPE.

2 All of the following will increase the prevalence of racialized behavior in society _except_:
    a. increases in the average wealth of one's group.
    b. large numbers of persons acting as individuals rather than as group members.
    c. increases in income inequality between groups.
    d. all will increase the prevalence of racialized behavior.

3. Collective racial identity has all of the following properties *except*:
   a. it is a quasi-kinship based affiliation.
   b. it is created by other productive activities.
   c. it is unrelated to governmental specification of rules of racial classification.
   d. it is a public good for those who identify with the identity.
4. Economies of scale in cultural identity production can enable the establishment of all of the following *except*:
   a. black churches.
   b. independent black schools.
   c. black-owned businesses.
   d. the establishment of all of these can be facilitated if economies of scale in cultural identity production exist.
5. Cultural production externalities are important in all of the following *except*:
   a. marriage markets.
   b. employment in positions with high levels of prestige and power.
   c. religious observances.
   d. cultural production externalities are important in all of these activities.
6. According to the 2000 federal decennial census:
   a. about 98 percent of whites selected "white" as their sole racial identity and about 2 percent selected "white" and at least one other racial category.
   b. about 94 percent of whites selected "white" as their sole racial identity and about 6 percent selected "white" and at least one other racial category.
   c. about 2 percent of whites selected "white" as their sole racial identity and about 98 percent selected "white" and at least one other racial category.
   d. about 6 percent of whites selected "white" as their sole racial identity and about 94 percent selected "white" and at least one other racial category.
7. According to the 2000 federal decennial census:
   a. about 98 percent of blacks selected "black" as their sole racial identity and about 2 percent selected "black" and at least one other racial category.
   b. about 94 percent of blacks selected "black" as their sole racial identity and about 6 percent selected "black" and at least one other racial category.
   c. about 2 percent of blacks selected "black" as their sole racial identity and about 98 percent selected "black" and at least one other racial category.
   d. about 6 percent of blacks selected "black" as their sole racial identity and about 94 percent selected "black" and at least one other racial category.
8. Collective economic interests among African Americans originate:
   a. from the ideology of white racial superiority and economic rents generated at the expense of white Americans.
   b. from the ideology of white racial superiority and wide access to economic rents generated at the expense of African Americans and other nonwhite groups.
   c. from the ideology of white racial superiority and common patterns of oppression experienced by individuals during different historical periods from the era of slavery until the present.
   d. from the communal traditions of African societies and common patterns of oppression experienced by individuals during different historical periods from the era of slavery until the present.

9. Collective racial identity emerges as a social norm:
   a. when a critical mass of individuals finds that it is in their individual interests to engage in own-group altruism and other-group antagonism.
   b. only if the government establishes rules, institutions, and forms for identifying and sorting persons according to skin color.
   c. when individualism offers a superior strategy for increasing income and wealth.
   d. when a person's income or wealth is independent of group affiliation.

10. Over time, we may observe that racialized behavior spreads from a critical mass of persons (which may be a numerical minority) to the overwhelming majority of persons in a society:
    a. when persons of different skin colors do not have compatible cultures, behaviors, and values.
    b. when the expected opportunity to obtain income and increase wealth are lower with individualism than with racialized behavior.
    c. when individualism offers a superior strategy for increasing income and wealth.
    d. only if the government initially establishes rules, institutions, and forms for identifying and sorting persons according to skin color.

11. Collective racial identity has characteristics that are similar to:
    a. negative externalities and public goods.
    b. positive externalities and public bads.
    c. externalities and public goods.
    d. positive externalities and public goods.

12. The BPE paradigm suggests that competitive market forces, in the long run, will:
    a. definitely erode collective economic action by racial groups.
    b. most likely erode collective economic action by racial groups.
    c. most likely reinforce racial identities.
    d. create a society where individuals are judged by the content of their character and not by the color of their skin.

13. Which of the following statements is *not* true?
    a. In the "taste for discrimination" model, an individual with a preference to discriminate is exercising an irrational preference.
    b. In the "taste for discrimination" model, racial discrimination is exogenously given.
    c. The concept of collective racial identity can be easily categorized and examined using standard economic theory.
    d. In the BPE paradigm, racial identity and racial cultural production develop from rational group and individual choices.

14. According to Becker's model, competitive market forces:
    a. weaken discrimination.
    b. strengthen discrimination.
    c. contain opposing tendencies to strengthen and weaken discrimination.
    d. play a minor role in the reproduction/nonreproduction of discriminatory practices.

15. According to Darity, Mason, and Williams, competitive market forces:
    a. weaken discrimination.
    b. strengthen discrimination.
    c. contain opposing tendencies to strengthen and weaken discrimination.
    d. play a minor role in the reproduction/nonreproduction of discriminatory practices.

16. Which of the following is *not* a significant feature of the BPE paradigm?
    a. Structural changes in the economy can have a significant impact on the balance of power between dominant and subordinate groups.
    b. Racial stratification processes facilitate the assignment of high-level jobs to members of the dominant racial group.
    c. Racism is deeply embedded in the normal functioning of the U.S. political economy.
    d. Government interventionist policies forced by the civil rights movement were designed to create a more equitable, less racial distribution of wealth.

17. Which of the following statements is *not* true?
    a. More than 70 percent of the white population believes that less qualified blacks get jobs or promotions before more qualified whites do.
    b. More than 70 percent of the white population believes that less qualified blacks get admitted to colleges or universities ahead of more qualified whites.
    c. About 25 percent of low-income workers have access to employer-sponsored pension plans.
    d. All of the above statements are *true*.

18. Spatial mismatch refers to:
    a. the mismatch between the supply of affordable rental units and the number of low-income households who need them.
    b. the mismatch between the supply of rental units in inner-city areas near the locus of employment opportunities (and freeways, reverse commutes, harbors, airports, and entertainment facilities) and the number of high income workers who want them.
    c. a situation in which blacks are physically distant from high employment areas as a result of the suburbanization of jobs and persistent racial segregation that has led to the concentration of blacks in inner-city areas with few employment anchor industries.
    d. a situation in which the number of job vacancies in a given inner city exceeds the number of qualified workers available to fill them as a result of urban revitalization.

19. Which of the following would not significantly contribute to the problem of spatial mismatch?
    a. A freeze on government funding earmarked for the construction of low-cost housing units in suburban areas.
    b. A rise in the number of "knowledge workers" seeking housing units in revitalized inner-city communities that are near clusters of high-growth, global corporations and key employment centers.
    c. An exponentially growing influx of Asian and Latin immigrants into the United States.
    d. A sharp rise in the incarceration rates of poor white men and women.

20. All of the following, in the BPE paradigm, are reasons why foreign-born workers are preferred over domestic black workers *except*:
    a. black identity production is perceived as having more negative externalities for whites than that of immigrants.
    b. status competition between blacks and whites is far more intense than that of immigrants and whites.
    c. immigrants possess relatively superior "basic traits" (e.g., self-initiative) that are valued in the labor market..
    d. immigration laws and residency status reproduce the conditions for relatively easy social control of immigrant workers.

Essay Questions

1. What are the major economic and social patterns that the black political economy (BPE) paradigm attempts to analyze and explain?

2. How does the analysis of the causes of interracial economic inequality using the BPE paradigm differ from analyses using traditional approaches?

3. Discuss the characteristics of racial identity that are incorporated into the BPE paradigm.

4. What types of evidence are used to support the interpretations of the dynamics of interracial inequality proposed by the BPE paradigm?

5. Use the key concepts incorporated in the BPE paradigm to illustrate how investments in racial identity can affect one of the following: (a) residential segregation, (b) choice of college, (c) likelihood of employment in high-status occupations, or (d) incarceration rates of black males.

Current Economic Status of African Americans
Hard Evidence of Racial Economic Discrimination and Inequality

PART IV PRESENTS recent data on racial inequality and racial discrimination in labor and financial markets. Racial inequality in economic well-being exists when there are racial differences in economic outcomes such as income, wealth, employment, housing, access to credit, and so forth. Racial discrimination exists when otherwise identical persons are treated differently because of their race. Increasingly, public policy and popular discussion appear to be guided by the notion that racial discrimination within financial and labor markets has all but disappeared. Indeed, it has become fashionable among both conservatives and liberals to argue that racial inequality in outcomes merely reflects racial differences in individual behavior, family values, and community norms. Despite the conventional wisdom to the contrary, the chapters in this section show that racial economic inequality is not a function of dysfunctional behavior among African Americans. Rather, racial discrimination in labor and financial markets is responsible for a substantial portion of racial differences in economic outcomes. Moreover, because this discrimination has persisted for a substantial period of time, it calls into the question the social justice of past and present economic policies, as well as the capacity of competitive markets to create equal opportunity for all Americans.

Susan Williams McElroy's, "Race and Gender Differences in the U.S. Labor Market: The Impact of Educational Attainment," discusses the relationship between years of education and three important labor market outcomes: labor force participation rate, unemployment rate, and annual earnings for year-round, full-time workers. Regardless of race or gender, the labor force participation rate increases with years of education. Notably, within educational categories, African American and Hispanic women have higher labor participation rates than white women and Hispanic males have higher rates than white males. The largest African American–white male gap is for high school dropouts, where the labor force participation rate for African American men is 47 percent while it is 57 percent for white males.

McElroy also demonstrates that the unemployment rate goes up as years of education go down. African American and Hispanic unemployment rates for persons without a college degree are higher than the white rate; indeed, the unemployment rate for African Americans is twice the rate for whites.

Annual earnings also increase with years of education. Racial differences are largest for males. White male college graduates have the highest annual earnings. Black male college graduates have the lowest earnings for males with college degree. Black and white female college graduates have similar wages but both have lower earnings than similarly educated men.

Patrick L. Mason's "Persistent Racial Discrimination in the Labor Market" makes the point that competitive markets are not sufficient to destroy racial discrimination within the labor market. During the "Nadir," that is, 1877 to World War I, racial inequality in occupational prestige increased as racial inequality in literacy declined. During the current period, 1974 to the present, racial inequality in weekly wages increased as racial inequality in the quality and quantity of schooling declined. These circumstances strongly suggest that groups and individuals concerned with eliminating discrimination in labor markets should not accept the complacent conceit of conservatism that competitive markets will automatically end racial discrimination in the labor market.

Mason also shows that African American male access to employment declined substantially during 1964–2000, with the employment-population ratio falling from 74 percent to 63 percent. However, African American female access to employment increased from 48 percent to 62 percent—even as the employment-population ratio for white women rose from 45 percent to 69 percent.

Turning to financial markets, Gary A. Dymski and Patrick L. Mason's, "Racial Inequality and African Americans' Disadvantage in the Credit and Capital Markets," reports that African Americans have a 60 percent higher chance of being denied credit than otherwise identical white loan applicants. Furthermore, redlining—the practice of limiting the supply of credit to racial minority communities—is a continuing problem in financial markets. Among other things, the authors conclude that the Community Reinvestment Act needs to be extended to cover mortgage companies, finance companies, and nonbanking financial institutions. These institutions (along with commercial banks) pull savings out of black communities but do supply loans back to community residents. Apparently, it is also the case that competitive markets are not sufficient to eliminate discrimination and redlining in financial markets—just as competitive markets are not sufficient to eliminate racial discrimination in labor markets.

The next two chapters explore the distinctive experiences of African American women as they seek to ensure not only their own survival but also that of their children. Cecilia A. Conrad's "Changes in the Labor Market Status of Black Women, 1960–2000," describes the movement of black women into clerical and sales jobs after 1960, a change she attributes to the enforcement of equal employment laws, and the narrowing of the wage gap between black and white women, which she attributes to both legislation and improvements in educational attainment. Cecilia A. Conrad and Mary C. King's essay, "Single-Mother Families in the Black Community: Economic Context and Policies," focuses on the status of one group of African American women—single mothers who maintain families. The paper examines the economic and social factors contributing to the high proportion of black families headed by single women and the consequences for black families. Conrad and King emphasize the need for social policies to support families with children. Both selections highlight the economic burdens that fall on African American women as a result of the limited income-producing options for African American men.

Thomas M. Shapiro and Jessica L. Kenty-Drane's chapter, "The Racial Wealth Gap," shows that the African American–white wealth ratio is 0.10; the median white net worth is $81,450 and median black net worth is $8,000. Subtracting out home equity, the numbers are $33,500 and $3,000, respectively. Fifty-five percent of African Americans and 25 percent of whites suffer from asset poverty, that is, these households do not have enough wealth for a family of four to live at the poverty level for three months. Wealth accumulation is related to inheritances, savings levels, and income, and white households far outpace African American households in all three areas. Hence, the racial wealth gap is likely to persist far into the future. Indeed, since the racial gap in years of education is relatively small, both current and future racial inequality is strongly linked to the racial gap in wealth. If we are unable to structure the U.S. political economy in a way to substantially reduce inequality in wealth, then racial economic inequality and racial conflict will be with us for many generations to come.

4. Using the data in this selection, substantiate the claim that "Differences in educational attainment provide little insight into gender differences in labor force participation and unemployment rates."

5. Define the terms "occupation" and "occupational distribution." From the evidence in this chapter, what can we infer about the occupational distribution of race–gender groups?

Additional Essay Questions

6. What historical reasons can you give for the fact that women have a lower labor force participation rate than men? For the fact that black women have a higher labor force participation rate than white women?
7. Why might the reported data distinguish between individuals with some college and no degree, rather than distinguishing between individuals based on years of education?
8. Why might workers with at least a bachelor's degree, who are not non-Hispanic white males, have a smaller race-gender earnings gap than workers of similar background who lack a bachelor's degree?

2. Summarize the changes in black women's labor market status between 1980 and 2000 and compare this to the experience of white women workers.

3. Between 1960 and 1980, the earnings gap between black and white women narrowed while between 1980 and 2000 it widened. Explain why.

4. Summarize and discuss the role of education in contributing to differences in the labor market status between black and white women.

5. Citing examples from the chapter, discuss the effect of racial discrimination on the economic status of black women.

2. Why is the prevalence of single motherhood of particular concern to the African American community?

3. What are the sources of high poverty rates for single-mother families in the United States?

4. E. Franklin Frazier, writing in 1939, asserted that slavery had impeded the development of monogamous, nuclear families in the black community. Do you agree or disagree? Cite evidence from the reading to support your argument.

5. Describe the impact that both the growth in the proportion of women who work outside the home and the narrowing of the gender wage gap have on the incentives for marriage.

Additional Essay Questions

6. William Julius Wilson argues that the high proportion of black families maintained by women is because of a scarcity of marriageable black men. What factors have reduced the supply of marriageable men? What are shortcomings of this hypothesis?
7. Which of the theories that attempt to explain the relatively high incidence of single motherhood amongst African Americans do you find most plausible? Why? (Be sure to support your choice with evidence.)
8. In your own words, describe why it is difficult to tell if there are negative consequences for children that result purely from growing up in a single-mother household, rather than from other associated issues such as poverty.
9. How might public policy improve the economic well-being of single mothers and their children? Propose at least two public policies and explain how they will affect the number of families maintained by women, the incomes of single-mother families, and child outcomes. Cite evidence from the readings to support your proposal.

5. Discuss the significance of inheritances for wealth accumulation. How do the "historical legacies" of the black community (such as slavery and segregation policies) affect the levels of inheritance in the black community?

Additional Essay Question

6. Given the obstacles to wealth accumulation in the black community discussed in the chapter, what actions might be taken by individuals and the government to increase levels of assets in black households?

Globalization and Its Impact on the Economic Well-Being of African Americans and Latinos

GLOBALIZATION, AND ITS two faces, has been changing communities in paradoxical and contradictory ways. On the one hand, it has been a powerful force in creating a new global village, characterized by increasing cooperation, cultural exchanges, and democratic practices among its inhabitants. This and other features of globalization have created new possibilities for the struggle against fear, ignorance, and white privilege. On the other hand, globalization has led to the spread of new social inequalities and intensified claims for racial privileges. The chapters in part V examine the impact of globalization on the socioeconomic well-being of people of color in the United States with particular attention to African Americans. Taken together, these chapters challenge the idea that all Americans significantly benefit from globalization and open up new ways of thinking about the struggle for black socioeconomic progress in the global era.

Peter Dorman's chapter, "Globalization, the Transformation of Capital, and the Erosion of Black and Latino Living Standards," gives an in-depth analysis of the impact of increased capital mobility on the economic well-being of black and Latino communities. He argues that the disappearance of key employment anchor industries and high wage jobs from these communities has been one of the main direct effects of increased capital mobility. Dorman's chapter further suggests that an indirect effect of increased capital mobility is the development of a new "profit paradigm" for business that has resulted in several negative social effects, including deunionization, more wage inequality, and contingent and insecure employment. Dorman shows that these trends have emerged with recent developments in the auto, textile, and apparel industries, and disproportionally burden black and Latino workers.

Mary C. King's chapter, "Globalization and African Americans: A Focus on Public Employment," points to a neat fit between globalization and recent conservative political policies by emphasizing the decline in the bargaining power of both governments and labor in the face of the kind of globalization we are experiencing. Greater corporate mobility has strengthened business pressure on government to lower taxes, cut services, and decrease regulatory oversight of corporations—which is directly opposed to the interests of the African American community as a whole. The shrinking public sector does seem to be employing fewer African Americans; blacks are now less overrepresented in government jobs than they have been, but this may indicate greater opportunities in the private sector than previously existed.

In the next chapter, "Immigration and African Americans," Steven Shulman and Robert C. Smith present an interesting twist to the analysis of the impact of globalization. Shulman and Smith draw on ethnographic and econometric studies to show that immigration into the United States is having a negative impact on the wages and employment prospects of U.S. minorities, especially African Americans. Their research also suggests that the growing number of immigrants entering the United States has intensified the competition for public services. Shulman and Smith interpret the international flow of labor in the same way that the other authors interpret international flows of capital and commodities: it increases competition and undercuts the economic security of American workers. Shulman and Smith's essay is certain to generate a great deal of controversy but is included in this volume because of its valuable contribution to the growing social research on the socioeconomic impact of immigration.

The last two chapters in this section analyze two of the most significant effects of the social crisis of globalization. In "African American Intragroup Inequality and Corporate Globalization," Jessica Gordon Nembhard, Steven C. Pitts, and Patrick L. Mason examine the ways that corporate globalization is creating unprecedented levels of inequality in the African American community. Their chapter starts out by defining corporate globalization and presenting hard data on increasing inequality among African Americans. It then provides an analysis of the causal relationship between key aspects of corporate globalization—including international trade and increased capital mobility—and growing African American intragroup inequality. The chapter ends by advocating several programs designed to lessen the adverse effects of globalization. In the last chapter of this section, "Globalization, Racism, and the Expansion of the American Penal System," Andrew L. Barlow argues that the rapid growth of African American incarceration rates is a manifestation of the social crisis of globalization. In Barlow's view, globalization is currently undermining the stability of the middle-class social order and the capacity of the state to redistribute resources downward. With limits on their ability to deliver entitlement programs to the poor and middle class, political elites have turned to criminalization as a way to bring "law and order" to dangerously polarized cities, and to ease the fears of middle-class whites.

CHAPTER

$\diamond$ **20** $\diamond$

Globalization, the Transformation of Capital, and the Erosion of Black and Latino Living Standards

Peter Dorman

Key Terms and Institutions

Capital mobility

Contingent work

Gini coefficient

Neoliberal globalization

Outsourcing

Reward effect

Sorting effect

Note: The true/false and multiple-choice questions below are ranked according to level of difficulty. For example, true/false questions # 1 and 2 below are less difficult than questions # 9 and 10.

True/False Questions

Indicate whether each of the following statements is True or False by placing a "T" for true or an "F" for false in the space provided.

_____ 1. The 1998 data on Michigan automotive suppliers show that on average skilled workers are paid more when they are not unionized.

_____ 2. The group that appears to have the largest wage benefit from unionization is Hispanic men.

_____ 3. According to data in the chapter, the industry with the fastest growth in outsourcing over 1974–1993 was chemical and allied products.

_____ 4. The sorting effect and the reward effect work in tandem to raise racial wage inequality.

_____ 5. Urban black communities of the Midwest have achieved the highest living standards in their history in the 1990s economic boom.

_____ 6. Differences in income between whites and minorities are larger than their differences in financial wealth.

_____ 7. As the large car firms have increased market share in recent years, they account for an increasing share of the automotive workforce.

_____ 8. Dorman argues that low wage workers in foreign nations need to unionize so that minority living standards in the United States can improve.

_____ 9. According to Dorman's viewpoint, a tax on capital movement would be expected to raise minority living standards.

_____ 10. Evidence on income inequality using the gini coefficient contradicts evidence from the standard deviation of the wage distribution.

Multiple-Choice Questions

Circle the letter that corresponds to the (one) best answer.

1. According to table 20.2, the number of Latino workers employed in the U.S. apparel industry fell between 1979 and 1999 because:
   a. they were displaced by black workers.
   b. there was an overall decline in employment in that industry.
   c. their share of overall employment decreased.
   d. the size of the Latino labor force declined.

2. Looking at racial wage inequality during the past twenty years as a function of sorting and reward effects shows:
   a. that increased inequality is a result of increased differences in access to good jobs.
   b. that increased inequality is a result of increased differences between the wages paid in good and bad jobs
   c. that affirmative action programs have succeeded in reducing the economic gap between white and black workers.
   d. that affirmative action programs have made no difference in the economic gap between white and black workers.

3. Until the late 1970s, the main strategy pursued by U.S. businesses was:
   a. finding the cheapest sources of labor.
   b. breaking up into small units to maximize flexibility.
   c. safeguarding long-term investments through organizational size and stability.
   d. eliminating all labor unions.

4. Affirmative action in employment tends to:
   a. minimize the reward effect; i.e., different payment for different jobs.
   b. reduce the sorting effect by increasing the proportion of people of color in better paying jobs.
   c. have little effect on wages of blacks relative to whites.
   d. reduce capital mobility.
5. Capital mobility has caused increased wage inequality by all of the following *except*:
   a. increasing part-time and temporary workers.
   b. giving workers more choice of where to work.
   c. decreasing unionization.
   d. increasing job insecurity and job displacement.
6. The increased racial wage gap in the auto industry can be traced to:
   a. overt racial discrimination by the Big Three auto companies.
   b. overt racial discrimination by the United Automobile Workers union.
   c. wider pay differentials at the top tier employers.
   d. the effect of increasingly nonunion supplier production on jobs disproportionately held by black workers.
7. Studies using a two part method to look at inequality find that:
   a. racial inequality plays a large role in wage inequality.
   b. residuals point to government policies that hinder equality.
   c. wage inequality is mostly caused by factors among groups with the same demographics.
   d. wage inequality is mostly due to differences in education.
8. Beginning in the late 1970s, U.S. businesses adopted a new strategy based on:
   a. ending long-term commitments to workers, locations, and particular products.
   b. forming partnerships with unions to achieve greater efficiency.
   c. creating larger and more coordinated systems of organization.
   d. maintaining production in the United States in the face of foreign competition.
9. Changes in the auto industry have caused a decrease in the wages of black autoworkers by:
   a. decreasing employment of black workers.
   b. decreasing employment and wages in the firms producing auto parts.
   c. lowering wages and employment in the Big Three: General Motors, Ford, and Chrysler.
   d. weakening unionization in the Big Three.

Essay Questions

1. How have changed economic conditions encouraged firms to switch from the old to the new profit paradigm? In other words, why did this change occur during the late 1970s and 1980s, rather than during the 1950s or 1960s?

2. What has been the effect of declining membership in unions on black and Latino men, and on black and Latino women?

3. The chapter focuses on the disadvantages for black and Latino communities of the change in business strategy. Can you think of any positive aspects of this change for minority communities in the United States? What about for other groups besides the owners and managers of these companies?

4. Define capital mobility and then explain its effects on racial inequality.

5. What reasons, other than racial discrimination, might cause minorities to be over-represented in contingent work? Is the overrepresentation a problem for society? Why or why not?

Additional Essay Questions

6. The civil rights movement has historically been more directed at sorting inequality than rewarding inequality. What strategies might the movement employ today to address the growing inequality in rewards? What strategy is suggested by Peter Dorman to further racial equality?

7. Do you think that unions provide or cause job training to be provided for their employees? Why or why not? What would be the implication for Dorman's union wage premium argument if this were true?

8. Analyze what has been happening in the auto, textile and garment industry over the last 25 years and what has been its impact on black and Latino communities. The chapter claims that traditional political strategies employed by civil rights groups are less effective today at overcoming racial inequality in the economy. Research one of these movements, such as the unionization efforts of Bayard Rustin, Jesse Jackson's Operation PUSH, or Cesar Chavez' United Farm Workers. What additional barriers would/do these movements face today because of global capital mobility?

CHAPTER

21

Globalization and African Americans: A Focus on Public Employment

Mary C. King

Key Terms and Institutions

Agribusiness
Capital
Chief executive officer
Class
Current population survey
Economic globalization
Marxist economists

"The Pie"
Private sector
Public employment
Public sector
Public services
U.S. wage structure

Key Names

John Bound
Lynn Burbridge
William Carrington
Jacqueline Jones
Mary C. King
Robert Lieberman

Lawrence Mishel
Melvin Oliver
Jill Quadagno
Ronald Reagan
Dani Rodrik
Thomas M. Shapiro

True/False Questions

Indicate whether each of the following statements is True or False by placing a "T" for true or an "F" for false in the space provided.

_____   1. There is evidence that the racial wage gap appears to have declined over the 1999–2001 period.
_____   2. Since 1980 the fraction of Americans who work in government jobs has been rising.
_____   3. African Americans are more likely to use public services than other Americans.
_____   4. Occupations in which women tend to be overrepresented are concentrated in the private sector.
_____   5. The real minimum wage is currently higher than at any time since 1968.
_____   6. Data in the chapter show that over the 1990s the overrepresentation of employed African Americans in the government sector declined.
_____   7. In 1990 about 20 percent of professional blacks worked in the private sector.
_____   8. The gender pay gap was larger among blacks than among whites in 2001.
_____   9. The data on earnings relative to white men show that since 1998 the public sector has reduced pay gaps by more than the private sector.
_____ 10. King's argument implies that restricting capital mobility would benefit black workers.

Multiple-Choice Questions

Circle the letter that corresponds to the (one) best answer.

1. Globalization, as it has occurred in recent decades:
   a. makes it easier for governments to tax businesses, because of improvements in communications and information.
   b. makes it easier for labor unions to bargain effectively with big corporations, because of improvements in communication between unionized workers around the world.
   c. makes it easier for business to bargain for lower taxes and wages, because improved communication makes it easier for them to relocate.
   d. makes it easier for journalists to expose business, labor, and government scandals, due to improved communication globally.

2. African Americans:
   a. have always had an easier time getting jobs from the government than from private employers.
   b. have been overrepresented in government employment since 1970.
   c. have always earned wages closer to those earned by whites in the private sector.
   d. face similar working conditions in both the public and private sectors.

3. African Americans, as a group:
   a. believe in self-sufficiency and so don't have much of a stake in the quality of public services.
   b. have often been discriminated against by the providers of public services and so don't have much of an interest in the funding for public services.
   c. are overrepresented among the public workforce and know from firsthand experience that public services primarily benefit the elderly.
   d. rely on public education, health, and other services and so have a community interest in maintaining good public services.
4. The year in which the pay gap was smallest between black men and black women in the private sector between 1992–2001 was:
   a. 1996.
   b. 2001.
   c. 1993.
   d. 1998.
5. Since the unemployment rate of African Americans is nearly always higher than that of whites:
   a. the data on earnings understate the racial income gap.
   b. whites have less need for public services.
   c. capital mobility has a greater impact on black employment than on whites.
   d. the data on government employment overstate the fraction of blacks in the labor force who work for the government.
6. African American women have been particularly overrepresented in government employment because:
   a. the government employs a lot of people in occupations that are traditionally "women's jobs."
   b. black women are not particularly concentrated in traditional "women's jobs," which are disproportionately found in the private sector.
   c. race has been more important than sex in determining where good opportunities occur for African American workers, and the Federal government has never discriminated on the basis of race.
   d. African American women are more likely than white women to be found in non-traditional jobs, like bus driving, police work, and the military.
7. The author thinks that the decreasing representation of African Americans among public sector workers:
   a. means that less-educated African Americans are losing out because their jobs are being "privatized."
   b. means that college-educated African Americans are obtaining more opportunities outside of government than in the past.
   c. both a and b.
   d. neither a nor b.

8. In comparing the receptiveness of the public and private sector to African Americans, it is accurate to say that:
   a. wages have been better for African Americans in the public sector, but the benefits have been better in the private sector.
   b. discrimination has been more pronounced in the public sector, but the opportunities for black professionals have been better than in the private sector.
   c. discrimination has been less apparent in the public sector, but wages are generally lower in the public than the private sector, particularly for more educated people.
   d. it's impossible to really compare the two sectors, as they employ such different categories of people.

Essay Questions

1. Why has the process of globalization thus far improved the bargaining power of business vis-à-vis both governments and labor?

2. Why do gains for business at the expense of government and labor probably mean losses—on average—for African Americans?

3. Describe in your own words the history of African American employment in the public sector in the United States.

4. How does employment in the public sector differ from employment in the private sector?

Additional Essay Questions

5. In your own words, why does the author of this chapter assume that the reduced overrepresentation of African Americans in the public sector in recent years means gains for blacks?
6. What reasons, besides those mentioned by King, might be responsible for the decline in the overrepresentation of African Americans in the public sector? Assuming the globalization trend continues, what should be done to help such workers transition into private sector work?

CHAPTER

22

Immigration and African Americans

Steven Shulman and Robert C. Smith

Key Terms and Institutions

Decennial census
Educational crowding-out
Ethnographic studies
Free market fundamentalism
IMF
Lingua franca

Means-tested programs
National ID card
Quantitative studies
Rainbow coalition
World Bank

Key Names

George Borjas
Frederick Douglass
Milton Friedman
Jesse Jackson

Barbara Jordan
Julius Simon
Thomas Sowell

Note: The true/false and multiple-choice questions below are ranked according to level of difficulty. For example, true/false questions # 1 and 2 below are less difficult than questions # 9 and 10.

True/False Questions

Indicate whether each of the following statements is True or False by placing a "T" for true or an "F" for false in the space provided.

_____ 1. Households with a foreign-born head are more likely to collect cash benefits such as food stamps and welfare.

_____ 2. Immigration is particularly harmful to African Americans since immigrants tend to compete with them for low-skilled jobs.

_____ 3. African Americans are often discriminated against in favor of immigrants of African descent.

_____ 4. Water's research shows that employers prefer immigrants over African Americans even when the immigrant is of African descent.

_____ 5. Immigrant networks pose problems for African Americans because in such workplaces Spanish is often the primary language.

_____ 6. The chapter suggests that, while ethnographic studies cannot establish the aggregate effects of immigration on African Americans, they can be useful in assessing the impact of immigration on the employment of African Americans in specific industries.

_____ 7. Census data from 1980 and 1990 statistically show that there is a negative link between immigration and the probability of high school graduation for blacks.

_____ 8. The primary argument against a national ID card is that it would harm civil rights.

_____ 9. Newt Gingrich and other conservative politicians have been outspoken in their opposition to immigrants.

_____ 10. Ethnographic studies provide conclusive evidence that immigration harms native workers.

_____ 11. Over the 1990s about 500,000 illegal immigrants settled in the United States each year, approximately triple the flow of the previous decade.

_____ 12. Borjas argues that, while immigration hurts African Americans, it produces net benefits for the economy as a whole.

_____ 13. It has been found that immigration increases government expenditures by about three times its increase in fiscal revenues.

_____ 14. The chapter suggests that ethnographic studies are more reliable than quantitative studies in assessing the overall impact of immigration on black economic well-being.

_____ 15. Overwhelmingly, the research cited in the chapter suggests that the net fiscal impact of immigration is negative.

_____ 16. Educational crowding-out refers to the fact that immigrants use voucher money on private schooling that would otherwise have gone to public schools with more minority students.

_____ 17. Following Smith and Shulman, it would not be unreasonable to conclude that immigrant employment causes more harm to African Americans in the long run than in the short run.

_____ 18. Immigration can benefit more highly educated African Americans since immigrants raise demand for their labor services.

_____ 19. The authors argue that black leadership should have little difficulty maintaining common ground with the advocates of free markets.

_____ 20. Reductions in legal immigration, as suggested by Barbara Jordan, would lower the incentives for Mexicans coming to the United States.

_____ 21. Measured effects of the impact of immigration may be biased upward because of labor supply and out-migration adjustments.

Multiple-Choice Questions

Circle the letter that corresponds to the (one) best answer.

1. The phrase "rainbow coalition" was associated with the supporters of presidential candidate:
   a. Bill Clinton.
   b. Jesse Jackson.
   c. George W. Bush.
   d. Al Sharpton.

2. Shulman and Smith's analysis implies that the recent rise of immigrants into the United States is primarily due to:
   a. the economic conditions of the countries from which U.S. immigrants are leaving.
   b. a desire to enjoy the liberty of being Americans.
   c. their eagerness to be with family already located in the United States.
   d. fears that they will be punished for criminal acts in their home nations.

3. Information cited on Latinos in the United States implies that:
   a. 80 percent of people of Mexican descent are in the United States illegally.
   b. border enforcement has recently lowered the number of illegal immigrants.
   c. they drain the economy since they send vast amounts of money to Latin America.
   d. only 1 in 5 Mexican immigrants are in the United States legally.

4. The authors advocate a national ID card system but which of their statements would lessen its impact?
   a. That they facilitate, but are not necessarily required for, transactions.
   b. Over 100 nations have national ID cards.
   c. Hispanic looking people would be singled out by that system.
   d. The cards are cheap and can be forged easily.

5. Aid provided to poor countries would have an adverse impact on low-wage workers in the United States if:
   a. it would lower the rate of immigration to the United States.
   b. the tax burden on American workers would rise.
   c. food imports from such countries could be safer due to reduced pollution.
   d. foreign markets would purchase more American goods.

6. Following Friedberg and Hunt's research, an increase in the immigration share of the population in a certain area in the 1990s from 17.2 percent to 23.7 percent would have decreased the wages of low-wage native workers in this area by _____ percent.
   a. 6.5%
   b. 6.9%
   c. 7.8%
   d. 8.5%

7. An argument that might be given to contradict the authors' viewpoint is that a "rainbow coalition" is likely to _____ a(n) _____ in the U.S. minimum wage.
   a. support; reduction.
   b. resist; increase.
   c. support; increase.
   d. ignore; change.

8. According to a study using data from New Jersey, how many percentage points of an increase in immigrants from Puerto Rico would cause African American wages to fall by 60 percentage points:
   a. 25.
   b. 10.
   c. 5.
   d. 15.

9. Several quantitative studies have shown a negligible impact of immigration on employment and wages of native workers. Which of the following is not discussed in the chapter as a reason why these studies and their findings of weak effects should be viewed with suspicion?
   a. The weak aggregate effects found in these studies may be explained by the possibility of offsetting (positive vs. negative) impacts on low-wage and high-wage workers.
   b. These studies use decennial census data and emphasize the substantial impact of immigration in the short run.
   c. These studies, in general, do not account for differences in local labor markets that can influence how immigration impacts low-wage native workers.
   d. All of the above are true.

Essay Questions

1. Describe the evidence for the argument that immigrants take educational resources away from native-born minorities. Do you agree with that position? Explain.

2. In what ways might immigration actually help African Americans? Explain.

3. What are the two types of studies of the impact of immigration on African Americans, and what do these studies show about the impact of immigration on the wages and employment of native workers?

4. Immigration primarily affects native workers who are high school drop-outs. Why?

5. Why do some studies of the impact of immigration on African Americans understate the actual impact?

Additional Essay Questions

6. What is the fiscal impact of immigration?
7. If immigration adversely affects African Americans, why have many African American leaders said so little about it?
8. What are some policies that can both benefit immigrants and reduce immigration? How can they accomplish both goals at the same time?

CHAPTER

23

African American Intragroup Inequality and Corporate Globalization

Jessica Gordon Nembhard,
Steven C. Pitts, and Patrick L. Mason

Key Terms and Institutions

Affirmative action
Civil rights movement
Corporate globalization
Deregulation
Environmental racism
General Agreement on Tariffs and Trade
  (GATT)
Gini coefficient
Income inequality
International trade
Intragroup inequality
North American Free Trade Agreement
  (NAFTA)

Percentile
Poverty
Quintile
Race-neutral policies
Trade adjustment programs
U.S. Census Bureau
United Automobile Workers
United Nations
Wealth inequality
World Bank

Key Names

William A. Darity Jr.
Peter Dorman
Jawanza Kunjufu
Clarence Lusane
Arjun Makhijani
Nelson Mandela
Patrick L. Mason
Samuel L. Myers Jr.

Jessica Nembhard
Melvin Oliver
Randolph Persuad
Thomas M. Shapiro
Rhonda Williams
William J. Wilson
Edward Wolff

True/False Questions

Indicate whether each of the following statements is True or False by placing a "T" for true or an "F" for false in the space provided.

_____ 1. Inequality is higher among black families than it is among white families.

_____ 2. Income inequality between industrial and developing countries tripled between 1960 and 1993.

_____ 3. About half of world trade occurs between one part of a transnational corporation and one of its subsidiaries, branches, or affiliates.

_____ 4. The authors argue that under corporate globalization, labor has become the most mobile factor of production.

_____ 5. U.S. income inequality has been rising since the late 1960s.

_____ 6. Nearly 33 percent of African Americans have negative wealth or no wealth.

_____ 7. African Americans outside of the South have a higher rate of home ownership than Southern blacks.

_____ 8. Free trade agreements have benefited African Americans.

_____ 9. Poverty rates of black families are negatively correlated with economic growth.

_____ 10. Gini coefficient measures changes in income.

_____ 11. The decline in the demand for low-skilled labor has hurt whites more than blacks because whites are less skilled on average.

_____ 12. On average white households hold more than 6 times the financial wealth of African American households.

_____ 13. The authors claim that the negative impacts of corporate globalization can be counteracted with policies to improve worker productivity and labor demand.

_____ 14. Between 1974–2000, income inequality within the African American community increased.

_____ 15. In 2000 the top 5 percent of black families in the income distribution controlled 7 times as much income as the bottom quintile.

_____ 16. In 1997 the 200 largest transnational firms controlled about 35 times more percentage points of the world's Gross Domestic Product (GDP) than it employed of the world's workforce.

_____ 17. Trade can explain about two thirds of the decline in employment in ten trade impacted concentrated industries over 1976–1985.

_____ 18. Over 1979 to 2000 African Americans became more likely to have an employer with a pension plan.

Multiple-Choice Questions

Circle the letter that corresponds to the (one) best answer.

1. The globalization of today is called "corporate globalization" because:
   a. the past thirty years is the only time that corporations existed.
   b. transnational corporations make the rules, benefit from, and control most of the globalization.
   c. while the U.S. government determines the rules of globalization, corporations gain the most.
   d. transnational corporations make the rules of globalization even though they are not the chief beneficiaries.

2. Between 1975 and 1996, the wage differences among the top exporting countries:
   a. stayed the same.
   b. fell due to increased competition.
   c. increased from a ratio of about 2.5:1 to a ratio of 103:1.
   d. decreased because governments began to restrict the movement of corporations.

3. When one examines the data on income inequality among African Americans evidence shows that:
   a. the Gini ratios tell a different story as the numbers that compare the incomes of the richest and poorest quintiles.
   b. it increased between the mid-1960s to today.
   c. it fell since the mid-1960s.
   d. it increased between the mid-1960s to the early 1990s and then fell slightly since then.

4. When one examines the data on poverty among African Americans:
   a. poverty rates for African American families were lower in 1970 than in 2000.
   b. poverty rates rise during recessionary periods.
   c. poverty rates among African American single-parent households are the same as poverty rates among African American married couples.
   d. poverty rates among African American families rose during the expansion years of the 1990s.

5. When examining the impact of trade on African American employment:
   a. the percentage of African American workers employed in manufacturing rose from 1985 to 2000.
   b. the industries most impacted by NAFTA are those industries where there is a concentration of African American workers.
   c. any job loss by African Americans did not impact income inequality within the Black community.
   d. as globalization changed the demand for labor from unskilled to skilled labor, this change did not affect African Americans.

6. During the generation between the middle 1970s and the middle 1990s, inequality between African American families:
   a. increased because international trade created many high wage manufacturing jobs for less educated male workers.
   b. increased because international trade created many high wage manufacturing jobs for prime-aged males.
   c. increased because international trade eliminated many high wage manufacturing jobs for less educated prime-aged males.
   d. increased because international trade eliminated many high wage service jobs for more highly educated prime-aged males.

7. The period from 1964 to 2000 witnessed great changes in inequality. In particular,
   a. there was an expansion in the fraction of middle-class African American and white families.
   b. there was an expansion in the fraction of middle-class white families, but racism continued to hold back an increase in the fraction of African American families.
   c. there was an expansion in the fraction of middle class African American families and an expansion in the fraction of elite and upper income African American families because lower income and very poor African American families decreased.
   d. there was a decline in the fraction of middle class African American and white families.

8. Which of the following Gini coefficients indicates the greatest degree of income equality?
   a. 1.0
   b. 0.6
   c. 0.4
   d. 0.2

9. From 1982–1985, the black Gini coefficient:
   a. decreased.
   b. increased.
   c. remained the same.
   d. was equal to the white Gini coefficient.

10. Which of the following statements is *true*?
    a. Within-race income inequality has declined significantly since the late 1970s for both blacks and whites.
    b. Within-race income inequality has declined significantly since the late 1970s for blacks but not for whites.
    c. Within-race income inequality has increased significantly since the late 1970s for whites but not for blacks.
    d. Within-race income inequality has increased significantly since the late 1970s for both blacks and whites.

11. Among the industries listed in the chapter as trade impacted manufacturing industries, which saw the largest percentage decline in black employment between 1985–2002?
    a. Glass.
    b. Ships and boats.
    c. Construction equipment.
    d. None of the above.

Essay Questions

1. Define corporate globalization. Discuss at least five characteristics of twenty-first-century globalization. How do major corporations control world trade?

2. What is the difference between intergroup and intragroup level analysis? Why is it important to document and understand increasing economic inequality? Why is it important to understand African American intragroup economic inequality in the twenty-first century?

3. Discuss at least two ways to measure income inequality. How do they show the dwindling of the black middle class? What is the significance of this?

4. Examine Figure 23.1 and Table 23.1. What do they tell us? How is the information similar and dissimilar between the two types of graphic presentation? Does one format show income inequality better than the other? If so, why? If not, why not?

5. Discuss trade-related job loss over the past 20–30 years. Which manufacturing industries have lost the most number of black jobs between 1985 and 2002? How has trade-related job loss affected African Americans? How has it affected inequality among African Americans?

Additional Essay Questions

6. Discuss at least three different indicators that when analyzed show increasing economic inequality within the African American community. Explain the three indicators and how they are calculated. How do they show increasing inequality? Are there other better ways to document economic inequality? Explain.
7. Describe the differences between wealth and income—what are the components of each? What do we learn by comparing black and white income levels? What do we learn by comparing black and white wealth holdings? Explain how wealth inequality explains black/white differences in economic status and black/black (intragroup) inequality. Use some specific components of wealth in this discussion.
8. Discuss some of the solutions to the undesirable affects of corporate globalization. Which ones seem most feasible? Which ones are more difficult to accomplish? Which solutions or strategies do you find most viable?

CHAPTER

24

Globalization, Racism, and the Expansion of the American Penal System

Andrew L. Barlow

Key Terms and Institutions

Disenfranchise

Prison-industrial complex

"Three strikes" laws

Transnational corporations (TNCs)

White flight

Willie Horton ads

Key Names

William Chambliss

Michael Dukakis

Note: The true/false and multiple-choice questions below are ranked according to level of difficulty. For example, true/false questions # 1 and 2 below are less difficult than questions # 9 and 10.

True/False Questions

Indicate whether each of the following statements is True or False by placing a "T" for true or an "F" for false in the space provided.

_____ 1. It has been estimated that 10 percent of black men have permanently lost the right to vote due to felony convictions.

_____ 2. U.S. crime rates have generally been rising since the 1970s.

_____ 3. Politicians' dependence on the votes of the white middle class lead them to pander to fears about minorities.

_____ 4. Out of the pool of people who commit crimes, people of color are much more likely than whites to be arrested and incarcerated.

_____ 5. Racism in American society is the reason that politicians have supported criminalization and incarceration.

_____ 6. It is clear that the prison-industrial complex is a cause of prison expansion rather than simply resulting from it.

_____ 7. Most of the people who commit crimes are not charged or apprehended for their acts.

_____ 8. Aggregate government criminal justice expenditures have risen by less than 349 percent since 1982.

_____ 9. Willie Horton ads were shown frequently in the South in an effort to help George H. W. Bush become president.

_____ 10. Research finds that rural counties are justified in lobbying for prisons since such facilities help lower their unemployment rates.

Multiple-Choice Questions

Circle the letter that corresponds to the (one) best answer.

1. Latino men are _____ times more likely than white men to serve time in prison while black men are _____ times more likely than white men to be incarcerated.
   a. two; eight
   b. four; six
   c. four; eight
   d. five; nine

2. Which of the following are described as political targets used to exploit the fears of whites:
   a. Illegal immigrants.
   b. Muslim terrorists.
   c. Black criminals.
   d. All of the above.

3. The following are described as features of globalization in the most developed countries *except*:
   a. growing inequality.
   b. weakening of labor union power.
   c. reduced ability of the state to redistribute resources.
   d. increasing rates of immigration.
4. It is suggested that the growth of repressive force against communities of color is
   required to exclude minorities from accessing all of the following *except*:
   a. voting places.
   b. adequate housing.
   c. job education.
   d. social services.
5. If minorities make up 24 percent of the U.S. population then their incarceration rate
   implies that they are overrepresented by a factor of about:
   a. two.
   b. four.
   c. five.
   d. three.
6. The prison-industrial complex is more the _____ of prison expansion than the _____.
   a. bane; cure
   b. consequence; cause
   c. cause; consequence
   d. deviation; average
7. Globalization exerts a(n) _____ on the incomes of both middle-class whites and
   African Americans.
   a. positive influence
   b. upward pressure
   c. downward pressure
   d. hypnotic effect
8. The building of a prison in a rural community tends to _____ the local economy
   in that community.
   a. revitalize
   b. destroy
   c. cause a temporary economic boom in
   d. leave unemployment rates unchanged in

Essay Questions

1. Summarize the chapter's argument explaining the recent growth in the criminal justice system.

2. Explain the link the chapter makes between globalization and the American penal system.

3. Could resources be better utilized if our governments spent fewer funds on the criminal justice system? Explain.

4. What evidence is there for the claim that a "deeply structured racism in American society" exists?

5. Characterize the roles attributed to whites and African Americans in Barlow's chapter.

Additional Essay Questions

6. Are there ways in which globalization and the expansion of the American penal system might actually be aiding minorities? Explain.
7. Is there evidence that politicians who appear soft on crime are less likely to be supported by the electorate? Argue whether that is justified.
8. How might communities of color be able to counter the growth of criminalization and its negative impacts?

Black Capitalism:
Entrepreneurs and Consumers

PART VI EXAMINES the characteristics of black-owned businesses, from barbershops to hip-hop clothing manufacturers, and debates black capitalism as a strategy for black economic advancement. The chapters in this section identify several challenges to the viability of the black business sector, including black-owned businesses' shrinking share of the black consumer dollar, the small size and scale of most black-owned companies (especially black-owned banks), lack of access to capital and the demise of minority contracting and set-aside programs. Some authors are pessimistic about the potential of black business sector to have a significant impact on black employment and incomes. Others are cautiously optimistic. Some comparisons are made with businesses owned by members of other racial and ethnic minorities. Especially provocative are two chapters that address the links between popular culture and black wealth creation.

Manning Marable's "History of Black Capitalism" reveals that black-owned businesses thrived in an era of rigid racial segregation by providing goods and services to black consumers who frequently had few other options. However, since the 1960s, white corporations have begun to target the black consumer dollar. Marable argues that the net result has been a marginalization of black-owned businesses and black entrepreneurs. Cecilia A. Conrad's "Black-Owned Businesses: Trends and Prospects" is less pessimistic. Consistent with Marable's analysis, she documents a decline in the significance and size of the black business sector that caters to the black consumer market. However, she argues that government procurement and minority contracting programs spurred the diversification of black-owned businesses outside of this ethnic niche and that these new black-owned businesses experienced rapid growth during the economic expansion of the last decade.

Conrad describes how this recent growth has revived interest in black capitalism as a strategy for job creation in the black community. Black banks offer one example of a sector that emerged in the context of rigid racial segregation. Gary A. Dymski and Robert E. Weems Jr. ("Black-Owned Banks: Past and Present") document the exclusion of black consumers and businesses from bank credit and capital markets and the development of black banks as a response to this exclusion. They also assess the long-term viability of black banks in a financial environment increasingly dominated by a small number of large institutions. Drawing lessons from the experience of Hispanic and Asian American-owned banking sectors, Dymski and Weems conclude that black-owned banks can survive if they attain adequate scale through recruitment of new customers.

Two of the chapters in part VI examine aspects of hip-hop culture and its implications for black business development. Weems's "'Bling-Bling' and Other Recent Trends in African American Consumerism" focuses on excessive consumerism in some genres of hip-hop. He describes the simultaneous rise in black spending power and the decline of black consumer support of black-owned businesses. Acknowledging that the African American consumerism predates hip-hop, Weems singles out hip-hop's glorification of the acquisition of big cars, fancy clothes, and jewelry as emblematic of the failure of black consumers to patronize black-owned firms. As Weems notes, African American-owned companies "do not produce the items that promoters of bling-bling glorify." In "A Critical Examination of the Political Economy of the Hip-Hop Industry," Dipannita Basu questions whether hip-hop entrepreneurs are truly independent. Describing the complex economic relationships that comprise the hip-hop industry, she argues that many of hip-hop producers and labels are tied to large, multinational entertainment companies through distribution and other contracts. As a result, many lack control over their product.

Earl Ofari Hutchinson's chapter, "Black Capitalism: Self-Help or Self-Delusion?" raises doubts about the potential of black capitalism as a tool to generate employment and wealth for African Americans. Hutchinson worries that black capitalism will exacerbate class divisions among African Americans. He cautions that black capitalism by itself will not have a major impact on black economic well-being because of the small size of the black-owned business sector. The business success of other ethnic groups, such as Cubans and Koreans, cannot be used as a blueprint since these groups reflect selective immigration of well-connected, well-educated entrepreneurs. Hutchinson concludes that only the federal government can provide the resources needed to revitalize African American communities.

CHAPTER

25

History of Black Capitalism
Manning Marable

Key Terms

Black capitalism

Intermediate black petty entrepreneurs

Black corporate core

Proletarian periphery

Key Name

Booker T. Washington

Note: The true/false and multiple-choice questions below are ranked according to level of difficulty. For example, true/false questions # 1 and 2 below are less difficult than questions # 9 and 10.

True/False Questions

Indicate whether each of the following statements is True or False by placing a "T" for true or an "F" for false in the space provided.

_____ 1. Booker T. Washington was the founder of North Carolina Mutual Insurance Company.

_____ 2. There was a significant black slave-owning class in New Orleans prior to the Civil War.

_____ 3. According to Marable, desegregation permitted white corporations to develop a variety of strategies to make billions in profits from the black consumer market.

_____ 4. The "Golden Years" of black business occurred during a period of extensive racial segregation.

_____ 5. A relatively small number of black capitalists controlled a large percentage of the wealth generated by black businesses during the 1970s.

_____ 6. White control over the growing ghetto consumer market generated a significant political response from the black community.

_____ 7. The combined liquid assets of the corporate core of black capitalism is relatively small.

_____ 8. The black petty capitalist class made a few economic gains from racial discontent in the North from the 1930s to the late 1940s.

_____ 9. Black Entrepreneurship suffered during the period of Jim Crow segregation.

_____ 10. The white corporate strategy of gaining control of the black consumer market occurred first with a black-oriented advertising campaign by Coca-Cola in the early 1960s.

Multiple/Choice Questions

Circle the letter that corresponds to the (one) best answer.

1. The great migration North of blacks:
   a. contributed to a general movement of black businesses from the South to the North.
   b. led to Jewish, Irish, Italian, and Slavic business owners selling their business establishments to black entrepreneurs.
   c. led to a decline in Ku Klux Klan activities in the South.
   d. had very little impact on the growth of black firms in the North.
2. The origins of "black capitalism" can be traced to:
   a. the development of significant black finance capital after the Civil War.
   b. the development of a small black propertied class that emerged before the Civil War.
   c. the development of black cooperative enterprises in the North shortly before the Civil War.
   d. broad support from white Northern industrialists.
3. Black capitalism in the 1970s and 1980s may be separated in three distinct class formations:
   a. the proletarian periphery, the middle class, and the black capitalist class.
   b. the fundamental class, the subsumed class, and the periphery class.
   c. the black consumer class, the intermediate black petty entrepreneurs, and the black domestic core.
   d. the black corporate core, the intermediate black petty entrepreneurs, and the proletarian periphery.

4. "Black capitalism" is a concept that:
   a. traces its roots to the nineteenth-century African American struggle for civil rights.
   b. was reinvented in the 1980s by President Reagan.
   c. was emphasized in Booker T. Washington's program for black upward mobility.
   d. all of the above.
5. According to Marable, white corporations:
   a. give a significant amount of loans to black entrepreneurs.
   b. allow black corporations to exist for symbolic value alone.
   c. have a significant history of subcontracting with black-owned firms.
   d. oppose the development of black corporations.

Essay Questions

1. Describe the origins of "black capitalism."

2. Describe the major obstacles to the early formation of "black capitalism."

3. How did segregation affect black business development?

4. What impact did the Great Depression have on early black capitalism?

5. Describe and evaluate Marable's position on desegregation and black capitalism.

CHAPTER

26

Black-Owned Businesses: Trends and Prospects

Cecilia A. Conrad

Key Terms and Institutions

Afro-American Benevolent Society
Atlanta Life Insurance Company
Atlanta Mutual Association
Black Enterprise (*BE* 100)
Black capitalism
Black consumer dollars
Black consumer market
Board of Governors of the Federal Reserve
    System
Buy Black campaigns
Civil rights movement

Johnson products
Motown Industries
Minority set-asides
North Carolina Mutual
Office of Minority Business Enterprise
    (OMBE)
Survey of Minority-Owned Business
    Enterprises (SMOBE)
Traditional Black-Owned Business
    Enterprises
"Twenty by ten"

Key Names

Timothy Bates
Thomas Boston
Andrew Brimmer

Alonzo Franklin Herndon
Maynard Jackson
Madame C. J. Walker

Note: The true/false and multiple-choice questions below are ranked according to level
of difficulty. For example, true/false questions # 1 and 2 below are less difficult
than questions # 9 and 10.

True/False Questions

Indicate whether each of the following statements is True or False by placing a "T" for true or an "F" for false in the space provided.

_____ 1. In 1960, black-owned businesses were mostly small mom and pop operations, concentrated in retail sales and personal services.

_____ 2. The growth in black presence in retailing after World War I has been attributed to "Buy Black" campaigns.

_____ 3. According to a recent U.S. Census Bureau survey, less than 100 percent of black-owned businesses have paid employees.

_____ 4. Black-owned businesses had difficulty expanding beyond ethnic niches because white consumers would not patronize them.

_____ 5. The Public Works Employment Act of 1977 and the Omnibus Small Business Act created set-asides for minority contractors in public works projects.

_____ 6. Lack of financial capital is an obstacle to black business growth and development.

_____ 7. Black-owned businesses have a higher propensity to hire African Americans than do other businesses.

_____ 8. In 1997, the average black-owned firm was more than double the size of the average U.S. business.

_____ 9. President John F. Kennedy created the Office of Minority Business Enterprise in the Department of Commerce.

_____ 10. The concentration of blacks in activities such as shoe shines and funeral parlors is unrelated to the racial hierarchy in the post-Reconstruction United States.

_____ 11. Desegregation increased the size and importance of black-owned food stores, eating and drinking establishments, and personal service establishments.

_____ 12. Despite growth, the black-owned business sector represents less than one percent of total business receipts in 1997.

_____ 13. From 1977 to 1997, the percentage of black-owned firms serving the general open market increased.

_____ 14. Between 1977 and 1997, the proportion of black firms serving the national black consumer market to total black-owned businesses did not significantly change, even though during this same period the number of black firms selling to this market actually increased.

_____ 15. By 1997, less than 25 percent of black-owned firms served local black consumer markets.

_____ 16. The percentage drop in the number of black firms operating in the traditional black business sector between 1972 and 1992 cannot be determined from the information in the chapter.

_____ 17. The average annual growth rate in the number of black-owned firms between 1977 and 1997 was about 12.8 percent.

_____   18. The chapter suggests that, while desegregation had a positive impact on some black businesses, desegregation and related affirmative action policies tended, in the net, to hurt black business development.

Multiple-Choice Questions

Circle the letter that corresponds to the (one) best answer.

1. Alonzo Franklin Herndon founded:
   a. Johnson Publishing.
   b. Soft Sheen.
   c. North Carolina Mutual.
   d. Atlanta Life Insurance Company.
2. Within the general open market, the sector experiencing the greatest growth in share of receipts between 1977 and 1997 was:
   a. transportation.
   b. construction.
   c. human services.
   d. business services.
3. Cecilia A. Conrad's analysis suggests that the continued expansion of black-owned businesses will likely lead to:
   a. significant advances in employment creation for the black community as a whole.
   b. modest to negative net gains in improving the earnings of African American youth.
   c. the further misallocation of resources within the African American community.
   d. the further development of economic class divisions within the African American community.
4. In 1977, which company topped the *BE*100 list?
   a. Johnson Publishing.
   b. Johnson Products.
   c. Motown Industries.
   d. Philadelphia International.
5. Which of the following best describes changes in the industrial composition of black-owned businesses between 1944 and 1960?
   a. The industrial composition of black-owned businesses changed very little.
   b. There was extensive diversification among black-owned businesses.
   c. More white customers patronized black-owned businesses.
   d. Black-owned businesses became overrepresented in manufacturing.
6. Between 1977 and 1997, the total number of black-owned firms increased by:
   a. 240 percent.
   b. 356 percent.
   c. 312 percent.
   d. none of the above.

7. All of the following are contemporary obstacles to the expansion of black-owned businesses *except?*
   a. Government regulations that limit black businesses to black neighborhoods.
   b. Lack of access to financial capital.
   c. Small scale of businesses.
   d. Retrenchment in government set-aside programs.

8. The total sales of the *BE*100 grew by _____ percent (in thousands of 2002 dollars) between 1977 and 2001, which translates into an annual rate of about _____ percent.
   a. 730.2; 30.4
   b. 730.2; 29.2
   c. 630.2; 26.3
   d. 690.2; 28.8

9. Which of the following best describes changes in the industrial composition of *BE*100 firms from 1977 to 2001?
   a. The general open market's share of industry receipts decreased.
   b. The black consumer market's share of industry receipts increased.
   c. The biggest decline in sales occurred for large black-owned firms selling to the national black consumer market
   d. There were more firms in the music industry on the 2001–2002 list.

10. In 1960, the percentage of black self-employed eating and drinking establishments was about _____ percent greater than the comparable percentage for all businesses.
    a. 115.6
    b. 118.7
    c. 218.7
    d. 133

Essay Questions

1. What factors limited the expansion of black-owned businesses beyond niche markets before 1960?

2. Summarize changes in the industrial composition of black businesses from 1977 to 1997.

3. What was the impact of the civil rights movement on black-owned businesses?

4. What has been the role of government in the development and expansion of black-owned businesses? How has the role of government changed over time?

5. Do you think "black capitalism" can improve the economic status of African Americans? Cite evidence from the reading or others in this section to support your conclusions.

Additional Essay Question

6. Economist Andrew Brimmer questioned the wisdom of encouraging blacks to seek careers as self-employed businessmen rather than as managers in large corporations. What do you see as the advantages and disadvantages of one career path over the other?

_____

NAME

CHAPTER

27

Black-Owned Banks: Past and Present

Gary A. Dymski and Robert E. Weems Jr.

Key Terms and Institutions

1964 Civil Rights Act
Banko Popular
Binga State Bank
"Black capitalism"
Douglass National Bank
Federal Reserve
Freedman's Savings and Trust
    (Freedman's Bank)
Great Depression

"Great Migration"
Independence Bank
National Negro Convention movement
Panic of 1873
Savings Bank of the Grand Fountain
    United Order of True Reformers
Seaway National Bank
Small Business Administration (SBA)
U.S. Banking System

Key Names

Frederick Douglass
Abram Harris

Juliet E. K. Walker

Note: The true/false and multiple-choice questions below are ranked according to level of difficulty. For example, true/false questions # 1 and 2 below are less difficult than questions # 9 and 10.

True/False Questions

Indicate whether each of the following statements is True or False by placing a "T" for true or an "F" for false in the space provided.

_____   1.   Prior to 1865, blacks had no involvement in banking.

_____   2.   Freedman's Savings and Trust Company was the first bank to be organized and administered by blacks.

_____   3.   The regulations imposed by the Fed after the stock crash left minority communities with little or no access to banking services.

_____   4.   Only four African American banks survived the Great Depression.

_____   5.   Freedman's Bank assisted African American economic development.

_____   6.   A main contributor to the establishment of a black banking system was racial discrimination and the inability of blacks to access banking services.

_____   7.   Economist Abram Harris's book, *The Negro as Capitalist: A Study of Banking and Business among American Negroes*, describes the growth of black banks after World War II.

_____   8.   The Great Depression had little impact on black-owned banks.

_____   9.   Lyndon Johnson helped encourage black banking through his "black capitalism" initiative.

_____   10.   The Hispanic-owned banking sector is dominated by three large financial institutions and is highly centralized.

_____   11.   The rate of black bank formation was faster in the 1980s and 1990s than in the 1970s.

_____   12.   In order to survive, black-owned banks need to attain an adequate size.

_____   13.   Sophisticated economic models have proven that black-owned banks are less profitable than other banks.

_____   14.   Desegregation helped black-owned banks by making them more competitive in attracting white depositors.

_____   15.   Black-owned banks have stricter requirements when examining a black loan applicant than do other banks.

Multiple-Choice Questions

Circle the letter that corresponds to the (one) best answer.

1.   How many black-owned banks survived the Great Depression?
   a.   Twenty-one.
   b.   Eleven.
   c.   Six.
   d.   None.

2. After the failure of Freedman's Bank, how much of their savings was returned to depositors?
    a. None.
    b. Less than $20 per account.
    c. Half of their original deposit.
    d. All of their original deposit.
3. In which period is there evidence that the black banking system was growing faster than the rest of the banking system?
    a. 1898–1905.
    b. The 1950s.
    c. The 1970s.
    d. The 1990s.
4. Which of the following is a characteristic of the black-owned banking sector?
    a. It is dominated by two to three large financial institutions.
    b. It serves a national consumer base.
    c. It faces no competition from other banks for black depositors.
    d. Black-owned banks are somewhat less profitable than other banks.
5. Black-owned banks tend to be most successful when they:
    a. make risky loans.
    b. grow large enough to take advantage of economies of scale.
    c. locate in poor, underserved areas.
    d. prioritize aiding local community development over short-term profit.
6. To remain competitive, black-owned banks have used all of the following *except*:
    a. initiating conservative lending policies.
    b. taking advantage of small business loan guarantees.
    c. lowering interest rates to attract depositors.
    d. establishing partnerships with other banks.
7. An antebellum report argues that black's deposits at existing banks work to:
    a. improve their social standing by fostering saving.
    b. subvert their advance by aiding their antagonists.
    c. help create funds for the establishment of new business.
    d. keep interest rates at below market levels.
8. The banking industry's relations with blacks prior to 1900 would best be described as:
    a. exploitative.
    b. empowering.
    c. competitive.
    d. blithe.
9. In L.A. county heavily Asian American areas have about _____ times as many bank branches per capita as heavily black areas.
    a. two
    b. three
    c. five
    d. four

Essay Questions

1. How have the challenges of financing economic development in minority communities been changed by changes in the banking industry as of the 1980s?

2. What are the key principles for financing inner-city and minority communities' economic development? How can these principles be accomplished?

3. Discuss the importance of Freedman's Savings and Trust. Why did it have such a profound impact on the African American psyche? Can we still see its effects today?

4. Compare and contrast the experiences of blacks and other minorities in the United States in banking. What can black banks learn from the experiences of other minorities?

5. In what respect must black banks balance "lending risk versus community service"?

6. What are the main issues confronting African American banks today and how do they differ from those that banks faced throughout their history?

Additional Essay Questions

7. What are some of the potential gains and limitations of using special programs to encourage more adequate financing of economic development in primarily African American communities?
8. How have changes in nationwide banking regulations affected African American banking?
9. How has suburbanization affected black-owned banks?

CHAPTER

28

"Bling-Bling" and Other Recent Trends in African American Consumerism

Robert E. Weems Jr.

Key Terms and Institutions

Bling-bling
Ceteris paribus
Emerge
Forbes
Rolex

Hip-hop
Madison Avenue
Minstrel shows
National Urban League
U.S. Census Bureau

Key Names

W. E. B. DuBois
Frederick Douglass

Tommy Hilfiger
Harriet Tubman

Note: The true/false and multiple-choice questions below are ranked according to level of difficulty. For example, true/false questions # 1 and 2 below are less difficult than questions # 9 and 10.

True/False Questions

Indicate whether each of the following statements is True or False by placing a "T" for true or an "F" for false in the space provided.

_____ 1. According to census data, African Americans, between the years 1996–2001, spent over $100 billion more on clothing than they spent on books, computers, computer-related equipment, and education.

_____ 2. Corporate marketers are believed to exploit the status anxiety of African Americans.

_____ 3. Because of the huge amount of money African Americans have spent buying his products, Tommy Hilfiger has always shown black consumers the utmost respect.

_____ 4. Since the advent of bling-bling, the wealth gap between blacks and whites has narrowed significantly.

_____ 5. African American consumer spending associated with bling-bling has proved profitable to black-owned businesses.

_____ 6. Hip-hop, from the beginning, consciously promoted African American consumption of "name brand" and luxury items.

_____ 7. Nearly one-half of the African American consumer market was under the age of eighteen in 1999.

_____ 8. Because of tight economic times, the buying power of African Americans declined between 1996–2001.

_____ 9. There appears to be a link between African American employment patterns and African American consumption.

_____ 10. According to census data, African Americans, between the years 1996–2001, spent almost as much money on alcoholic beverages, tobacco products, and smoking supplies as they spent on books, computers, computer-related equipment, and education.

_____ 11. Between the years 1996–2001, African Americans spent a total of $38 billion dollars on insurance. Of this total, 10 percent, or nearly $4 billion dollars, was spent with African American insurance companies.

_____ 12. In 1997 only 1 percent of black-owned businesses had 100 or more employees.

Multiple-Choice Questions

Circle the letter that corresponds to the (one) best answer.

1. Which of the following items are *not* generally associated with bling-bling?
   a. Jewelry.
   b. Gold and platinum plated teeth.
   c. Stocks and bonds.
   d. Fancy/expensive motor vehicles.

2. In Billy Tidwell's important 1988 essay, "Black Wealth: Facts and Fiction," he noted that although African Americans represented approximately 10 percent of the U.S. population, their (African Americans) total net worth was what percentage of the total?
   a. 13.3 percent.
   b. 7.1 percent.
   c. 2.8 percent.
   d. 0.9 percent.
3. Name the former editor of *Emerge* magazine who wrote an important essay, describing contemporary African American consumerism, entitled "Walking Billboards":
   a. George Curry.
   b. Kevin Powell.
   c. Earl C. Graves.
   d. John H. Johnson.
4. Out of 823,499 total African American-owned businesses, according to the 1997 survey of black business in America, how many had more than 100 employees?
   a. 50,000.
   b. 889.
   c. 26.
   d. 2,818.
5. Between the years 1996 and 2001, the collective buying power of black Americans increased by _____ percentage:
   a. 75
   b. 61
   c. 38
   d. 10
6. Data from 1993 reveal that if the black-white wealth gap were to close by 3 percent every five years then parity should be reached by:
   a. 2448.
   b. 2069.
   c. 2231.
   d. 2145.

Essay Questions

1. Census data indicate that African Americans spend much more money on alcoholic beverages, tobacco products, and clothing than they spend on books, computers, and education. What are the implications of this?

2. Do you agree or disagree with the author's contention that bling-bling ultimately works to the benefit of large white-owned companies (with little real benefit for blacks)?

3. Discuss the evolution of hip-hop from a phenomenon that promoted African American self-determination to one that serves as a "billboard" for the products of white corporate America.

4. Discuss the (economic) difference between buying fancy cars, clothes, yachts, and jewelry versus buying real estate, stocks, and bonds.

4. Do you think that African Americans can learn any lessons from the Jewish experience? Explain.

Additional Essay Questions

5. Describe Hutchinson's position on the role of the federal government in revitalizing African American communities.
6. Summarize and evaluate at least three of Hutchinson's strategies to make black businesses more competitive.

P A R T

Education, Employment, Training, and Social Welfare
Alternative Public Policy Approaches in the Struggle to Achieve Racial Equality

PART VII LOOKS AT current issues for public policies on education, employment, training, and social welfare with particular relevance for African American communities. The focus is a race-conscious analysis of policies ostensibly designed to provide "a hand-up" to the disadvantaged by improving primary and secondary education, reducing youth unemployment, finding the most effective training programs for low-wage workers, and "reforming" our social safety net.

Howard Fuller's chapter, "Black Power: The Struggle for Parental Choice in Education," makes the case that black parents should have the ability to choose a better education for their children, and that the best way to accomplish this is by public funding of vouchers for individual students to attend private school. Louis Schubert ("School Choice: A Desperate Gamble") responds by pointing out that voucher programs are never designed to pay the full cost of even relatively inexpensive private schools, so that only better off African American families can take advantage of them. He further emphasizes that the price of using public money to educate these students privately is to divert parents from demanding better public schools and to leave most students behind in classrooms with fewer resources but all of the expensive and difficult students that private schools can turn away. Schubert goes on to outline several possible strategies to improve our public schools, including smaller class sizes, more magnet schools, expanded cooperative programs with universities, increased faculty compensation, and outreach to parents to develop more parental involvement.

Michael A. Stoll's chapter, "The Black Youth Employment Problem Revisited," reviews what social scientists have learned from different programs designed to reduce youth unemployment, an issue of particular concern for African Americans, given the relatively low rates of employment of young black men and women. The most important research findings are (1) that employers favor young whites over young blacks in hiring, whether due to racism or to their perceptions—true or false—that black candidates' schooling and "soft skills" are not as strong as those of whites, and (2) that job growth is fastest in suburban areas difficult to reach by public transportation. Also the high rates of incarceration created by differential policing and the War on Drugs hurt many young people's job market prospects. Appropriate policy strategies include antidiscrimination efforts, strategies to make it easier for African Americans either to move or commute to job-rich locations, skill-building policies, and a change in our criminal justice policies.

Bernard E. Anderson's essay, "Employment and Training Solutions for the Economically Disadvantaged," examines the record of training programs over the last several decades, drawing several lessons. He finds that small positive impacts are possible for these programs, but that the best ones are difficult to replicate, depending perhaps on a particular conjunction of personnel and circumstances. Anderson asserts that public job creation is indispensable, because the market alone cannot fix the problem.

Linda Burnham's chapter, "Racism in U.S. Welfare Policy: A Human Rights Issue," analyzes the "welfare reform" of 1996 in the context of the extreme racialization of U.S. welfare policy historically. Income maintenance programs were structured to deny eligibility to African Americans, blocked by Southern senators until the mechanization of cotton (Allston and Ferrie 1993; Lieberman 1998; Lovell 2002). When welfare rolls "darkened," reflecting the disproportionate representation of African Americans and Latinos among the poor, a long-running political campaign helped to undermine public support for welfare by associating it with people of color. Burnham details the hardship that our miserly welfare system has worked, particularly on women and children of color, including increased homelessness and hunger.

The context for these discussions is the U.S. economy, neither "the best of all possible worlds" nor the only possible way to organize an economy. Obviously part of the U.S. context is racism, though perhaps not as powerful as it has been at other points in our history nor unique to us (Wilson 1978; Twine 1998). The other, too often neglected but extremely important, aspect of our economy is the unusual degree to which our government avoids using its power to ameliorate the worst effects of a market economy. The programs assessed in this chapter are much smaller than they could be, and smaller than similar programs are elsewhere.

The market economies of Europe produce as much poverty as does ours, but European governments act to soften the hard edges of markets (Mishel, Bernstein, and Boushey 2003). They put more resources into programs like the ones evaluated in this section, as well as providing more social services, income transfers, and mandating higher minimum wages (Freeman 1994). And far from stepping away from these strategies, social theorists for the European Union are looking toward expanding its "child-centered social investment strategy" as the only way to reduce adult poverty and unemployment in the future (Esping-Andersen et al. 2002).

Why are we different? It probably partly comes back to race. Many of the scholars focused on "American exceptionalism" say that we've been split by racial animosity, manipulated by those who want nothing but to keep their taxes low into thinking that social spending only benefits "them."

References

Allston, Lee J., and Joseph P. Ferrie. 1993. "Paternalism in Agricultural Labor Contracts in the U.S. South: Implications for the Growth of the Welfare State." *American Economic Review* 83 (4): 852–876.

Esping-Andersen, Gosta, with Duncan Gallie, Anton Hemerijck, and John Myles. 2002. *Why We Need a New Welfare State*. Oxford: Oxford University Press.

Freeman, Richard B. 1994. *Working under Different Rules*. New York: Russell Sage Foundation.

Lieberman, Robert C. 1998. *Shifting the Color Line: Race and the American Welfare State*. Cambridge, Mass.: Harvard University Press.

Lovell, Vicky. 2002. "Constructing Social Citizenship: The Exclusion of African American Women from Unemployment Insurance in the U.S." *Feminist Economics* 8 (2): 191–197.

Mishel, Lawrence, Jared Bernstein, and Heather Boushey. 2003. *The State of Working America, 2002/2003*. Ithaca, N.Y.: ILR Press.

Twine, France Winddance. 1998. *Racialism in a Racial Democracy: The Maintenance of White Supremacy in Brazil*. New Brunswick, N.J.: Rutgers University Press.

Wilson, William Julius. 1978. *The Declining Significance of Race: Blacks and Changing American Institutions*. Chicago: University of Chicago Press.

NAME

CHAPTER

31

Black Power:
The Struggle for Parental
Choice in Education

Howard Fuller

Key Terms and Institutions

Brookings Institution
Desegregation
Milwaukee Parental Choice Program
Milwaukee Public Schools (MPS)
National Assessment of Educational
   Process (NAEP)

Normal curve equivalent (NCE)
School boards
Teachers unions
U.S. Supreme Court
"White benefit"

Key Names

Kenneth B. Clark
Jay Greene
Sara Lightfoot

Tommy Thompson
Annette "Polly" Williams

True/False Questions

Indicate whether each of the following statements is True or False, according to the chapter, by placing a "T" for true or an "F" for false in the space provided.

_____   1. Less than 30 percent of public school teachers in the major cities of the U.S. enroll their children in private schools.

_____   2. Studies show that economic attainment is positively linked to a person's education.

_____   3. The core of the school voucher debate is about the power to make educational choices.

_____   4. Most African Americans are in favor of school vouchers.

_____   5. Teachers unions and parent organizations lead the forces against school vouchers.

_____   6. The Milwaukee Parental Choice Program was enacted in 1990 as a *place-based* program that targets places (e.g., the inner city) rather than as a *people-based* program that targets people (e.g., the homeless).

_____   7. The high school graduation rate of white students is 25 percentage points higher than that of black students.

_____   8. The 1970s desegregation plan in Milwaukee had a focus on helping minority children.

_____   9. There are studies that show that vouchers improve the educational performance of black children.

_____   10. Prior to entering the Milwaukee Parental Choice Program, program students were achieving above the level of other poor Milwaukee public school children.

_____   11. Prior to the voucher program in Milwaukee, only 4 percent of African American parents chose private schools.

_____   12. Milwaukee Parental Choice parents were more satisfied with the results of public schools than they were with those of private schools.

_____   13. The rate of school age children in private school is 35 percentage points lower than the private schooling rate for the school age children of Senators.

Multiple-Choice Questions

Circle the letter that, according to the chapter, corresponds to the (one) best answer.

1. The most controversial of the educational options available to parents are:
   a. charter schools.
   b. tax-supported vouchers.
   c. homeschooling.
   d. public-private partnerships.

2. The Milwaukee Public School (MPS) forced busing integration plan, as described in the chapter, was consciously designed to:
   a. spread the burden/social cost of desegregation equally across Milwaukee's black and white student population.
   b. places most of the burden/social cost of desegregation on Milwaukee's white student population.
   c. places most of the burden/social cost of desegregation on Milwaukee's black student population.
   d. mainly benefits Milwaukee's upper-income student population.
3. Among people reporting income, the median income of people without a high school diploma or GED is about _____ that of the median income of people with at least a high school diploma or GED.
   a. $10,000 less than
   b. twice
   c. $20,000 less than
   d. half
4. The Milwaukee Parental Choice Program was initially limited to:
   a. 341 children of brewery workers.
   b. 10,000 Milwaukee public school students.
   c. 1000 low-income students.
   d. 420 minority students.
5. Choice program students were found to gain _____ normal curve equivalent (NCE) points in reading and _____ NCE points in math after four years.
   a. ten; fourteen.
   b. five; six.
   c. thirteen; fifteen.
   d. six; eleven.
6. The following are true of the Milwaukee Parental Choice Program *except*:
   a. the number of students in the program has increased by about 7000 since 1990–1991.
   b. students in the program are from even lower income families than the typical low-income MPS family.
   c. the number of schools in the program has increased by a factor of more than 14 since 1990–1991.
   d. 81 percent of the participating students are minorities.
7. It can be inferred from the chapter that sponsors of the Milwaukee Parental Choice Program:
   a. wanted it to mainly benefit low- and middle-income families.
   b. wanted it to be without a target population.
   c. likely did not see a trade-off between increased publicly funded vouchers and improved performance in MPS.
   d. were mainly concerned with increasing black student performance in MPS.

Essay Questions

1. Summarize the weaknesses of the Milwaukee public schools desegregation plan of the 1970s.

2. Explain why the Milwaukee public school plan of the 1970s is essential to Fuller's argument.

3. Based on evidence from the chapter and your own knowledge, do you think tax-supported vouchers will be more prevalent in the future? Explain.

4. Public school educators and their supporters claim that school choice (vouchers) can harm black children. What arguments could be made in support of that claim?

Additional Essay Questions

5. The judiciary is an important actor in the chapter. Examine the impact that it has.
6. Describe the "black power" of the chapter's title. What groups are acting to limit that power.
7. The statement that "parental involvement, which was clearly high for Choice parents before they enrolled in the program, increased while their children were in private schools" could be problematic for the author's argument. Explain why or why not.
8. Fuller does not mention much about why students would perform better in private schools than in public ones. Describe some reasons based on your own education why you agree or disagree with that assessment.

NAME

CHAPTER

32

School Choice: A Desperate Gamble

Louis Schubert

Key Terms and Institutions

American Enterprise Institute
American Federation of Teachers
Black Alliance for Educational Options
Bradley Foundation
Brown vs. Board of Education
Children's Defense Fund
Democratic Party
Joint Center for Political and
    Economic Studies

Magnet schools
Milwaukee Parental Choice Program
NAACP
National Education Association
National Percentile Rating (NPR)
Public-private competition
Republican Party
School choice
School voucher

Key Names

George W. Bush
Milton and Rose Friedman
Howard Fuller
Al Gore

Jawanza Kunjufu
Charles Murray
Walton Family
Annette "Polly" Williams

True/False Questions

Indicate whether each of the following statements is True or False by placing a "T" for true or an "F" for false in the space provided.

_____   1. The best private schools charge less than $9,000 in yearly tuition.
_____   2. The conservative side of the voucher argument believes that government limits the people's freedom and harms the efficient allocation of resources.
_____   3. In the 2000 presidential election, 91 percent of African Americans voted for Democrat Al Gore.
_____   4. Young white males in elementary schools are disproportionately classified as having behavioral disorders.
_____   5. Low-income families have equal access to information needed to make good schooling decisions.
_____   6. Schools vary in quality largely due to differences in the amount of money per student that a school has available.
_____   7. The Milwaukee and Cleveland voucher systems tended to attract parents who were actively looking to aid their children's education.
_____   8. Teacher quality is the most important factor in student success.
_____   9. Advocates of school vouchers are attempting to associate them with poor urban blacks rather than rich whites.
_____   10. Private schools that accept vouchers are not allowed to discriminate among prospective students.
_____   11. The example involving Oakland, California, shows that nearby schools can have strongly different student performances.
_____   12. Most voucher programs propose funds that would give parents less than 40 percent of the cost of enrolling in the best private schools.
_____   13. The large overall support for vouchers among African Americans has more to do with practical considerations than ideological factors.
_____   14. Research cited in the chapter suggests, *ceteris paribus*, that improvements in black educational attainment resulting from lower class size would be greater than improvements from vouchers.

Multiple-Choice Questions

Circle the letter that corresponds to the (one) best answer.

1. It can be inferred from the chapter that:
   a. the improvements shown by voucher students will continue as such programs expand.
   b. African American support for school vouchers reflects their disappointment with the public school system.
   c. it is unlikely that public schools can be improved.
   d. improvements shown through vouchers are similar to the improvements that can be made with increased school discipline.

2. Among the factors not taken into account by voucher funds are each of the following *except*:
   a. the cost of textbooks.
   b. transportation costs.
   c. the costs of after-school programs.
   d. school lunches and breakfasts.

3. Which of the following is *not* described as one of the main factors determining the quality of public education in urban school districts?
   a. Academic magnet programs offered to secondary students in the city.
   b. The socioeconomic levels of parents in the school neighborhood.
   c. The difficulty of exams required to advance a grade level.
   d. The educational level of the parents in the school neighborhood.

4. Among the proposals to improve student success in public schools, the most important is:
   a. faculty compensation.
   b. cooperative programs.
   c. parental involvement.
   d. smaller classes.

5. Which of the following is *not* true of the support for vouchers among African Americans?
   a. The wealthiest families tend to support the conservative side of the debate.
   b. Overall support is at about 48 percent.
   c. Poor families are in strong support of voucher programs.
   d. Nearly two-thirds of those born between 1963 and 1972 favor vouchers.

6. The large support for school vouchers among African American reflects:
   a. growing support for the Republican Party among middle-income African Americans.
   b. a significant ideological shift among many African Americans toward conservative values.
   c. a and b above.
   d. none of the above.

7. All of the following are mentioned in the chapter as a problem with vouchers *except*:
   a. vouchers would reinforce existing inequities within the U.S. school system.
   b. vouchers would do very little to break down class- and race-based discrimination in the U.S. school system.
   c. a voucher system would be undermined by information imperfections that restrict a parent's ability to make rational school choices.
   d. the main beneficiaries of vouchers would be the wealthy.

8. Schubert's analysis implies that vouchers would produce:
   a. significant positive net benefits for black education as a whole.
   b. slight positive net benefits for black education as a whole.
   c. negative net benefits for black education as a whole.
   d. about zero net benefits for black education as a whole.

Essay Questions

1. Describe the groups that take the two sides of the school voucher debate.

2. Summarize the proposals to improve public schools.

3. Explain the argument that vouchers give unequal benefits.

4. What impact does parents' eagerness for quick improvements in education have on the debate between voucher programs versus improving public schools?

5. The author implies that voucher programs could lead to "abandoning over two centuries of American public education in favor of privatization." Do you agree with that assessment? Why or why not?

Additional Essay Questions

6. Aggressive adult education for parents is described as possibly being necessary to improve parental involvement. Explain whether you think that is feasible.
7. Is it fair that schools get the same amount of funds per voucher student regardless of the student's family income? Why or why not?
8. Using your educational experience as a guide, what methods of improving public schools were not discussed by the author? Describe the difficulties that such improvements would face.

3. Explain why the employment ratios of the 1990s are important for Stoll's argument. Is the movement in the gap among females problematic for that argument? Explain.

4. What other racial inequities may be present in the labor market that the chapter does not address? Explain.

5. Given the evidence in the chapter, what policies do you think would be best for addressing the labor market problems of black youth? Explain.

CHAPTER

Employment and Training Solutions for the Economically Disadvantaged

Bernard E. Anderson

Key Terms and Institutions

Adult training programs
Categorical programs
Center for Employment and Training
Comprehensive Employment and
    Training Act (CETA)
Demonstration project
Direct job creation
Dislocated Worker Initiative
Economically disadvantaged
Employment and training option
Employment Development for Youth
Empowerment zone
Enterprise zone
Four major programs
Job Training Partnership Act (JTPA)

Manpower Demonstration Research
    Corporation (MDRC)
National Research Council
National Supported Work Demonstration
    Project
Pilot projects
Public job creation
Urban poor
Urban poverty
Urban underclass
U.S. Department of Labor
War on Poverty
Welfare reform
Welfare-to-work programs

Key Names

Bernard Anderson   Richard Nixon
Daniel Patrick Moynihan

Note: The true/false and multiple-choice questions below are ranked according to level of difficulty. For example, true/false questions # 1 and 2 below are less difficult than questions # 9 and 10.

True/False Questions

Indicate whether each of the following statements is True or False by placing a "T" for true or an "F" for false in the space provided.

_____   1. Bernard Anderson's chapter focuses more on employment and training strategies that target people (e.g., the poor) than on strategies that target places (e.g., the inner city).

_____   2. Bernard Anderson's analysis implies that the conceptualization of the "rational self-maximizing individual" in standard economic theory does not apply to the urban poor.

_____   3. Past federal government efforts to improve the employment and training of economically disadvantaged groups have yielded limited positive results.

_____   4. Studies of past youth training programs reveal that these programs, without exception, show only negative to modest gains in improving the earnings of economically disadvantaged youth.

_____   5. All of the past four major federal government employment and training programs were designed, in one way or another, to address the problems of urban poverty.

_____   6. The statement "social science research supports continued experimentation with employment and training programs to improve the earnings of the urban underclass" follows from Anderson's terminology, discussion, and conclusions.

_____   7. According to the chapter, the reproduction of urban poverty is not the result of the cultural patterns of the urban poor.

_____   8. Past programs aimed at increasing the employment and training of urban, economically disadvantaged groups have targeted resources toward four major categorical programs.

_____   9. Summer youth employment programs targeted at low-income communities do not significantly increase the employment/population ratio for minority youth over time.

_____   10. In 1974, federal government employment and training policy shifted from categorical funding to the Job Training Partnership Act.

_____ 11. A weakness of the social science research studies cited by Anderson is that, collectively, they reveal very little regarding the benefits and limitations of the employment and training solution to the problem of urban poverty.

_____ 12. Bernard Anderson's analysis implies that competitive market forces do not benefit urban, economically disadvantaged groups.

_____ 13. The author claims that there is much room for experimenting with new programs aimed at improving the economic status of the urban poor since such programs were rarely explored in the past.

_____ 14. Over the past twenty-five years, the federal government and private foundations/institutions have played equal roles in the funding of efforts to increase the labor market participation of urban, economically disadvantaged groups.

Multiple-Choice Questions

Circle the letter that corresponds to the (one) best answer.

1. Bernard E. Anderson's analysis supports all of the following *except*:
   a. the continued experimentation with employment and training programs to address the needs of the urban poor.
   b. a free market approach to the economic problems of the urban poor.
   c. publicly funded economic incentives that advance locally-based, private-sector job creation.
   d. a public policy agenda that calls for steady, balanced economic growth.
2. Which of the following statements is *true*?
   a. Past social science research summaries examined by Anderson cover categorical programs, demonstration projects, and place-baced programs funded by federal, state, and local governments.
   b. Past public policy efforts aimed at increasing the employment and training of the urban poor include categorical programs, demonstration projects, and the Comprehensive Employment and Training Act (CETA).
   c. Past federal government programs designed to address the problem of urban poverty included adult training programs, welfare-to-work programs, and dislocated worker programs.
   d. None of the above.
3. Which of the following is not one of the four key lessons learned from social science research discussed in the chapter?
   a. Public job creation should be a part of comprehensive programs designed to improve the economic status of the urban poor.
   b. Limited but significant positive results are possible from the employment and training option.
   c. Strategies used by an effective employment and training program in a specific urban location can, in general, be successfully used in other urban areas.
   d. Market forces alone will not solve the economic problem of the urban poor.

4. Studies of past employment and training programs for adult men and women show:
    a. statistically negative results in improving the earnings of these two groups.
    b. no net gain in improving the earnings of these two groups.
    c. high positive net results in improving the earnings of these two groups.
    d. none of the above.
5. Bernard E. Anderson would likely agree with the view that current economic impoverishment facing many urban blacks can be strongly linked to:
    a. the dominant values and behavioral patterns of this group.
    b. the failure of this group to respond to economic opportunities.
    c. the lack of economic opportunities available to this group.
    d. the breakdown of married couple-headed families among urban blacks.
6. After 1974, federal employment and training policy encouraged:
    a. increased involvement of state and local government in the allocation of federal employment and training programs funds.
    b. increased involvement of the federal government in the allocation of federal employment and training funds.
    c. little change in the role of state and local governments in determining how federal employment and training funds would be allocated.
    d. increased involvement of the U.S. Department of Labor in the design of employment and training programs for urban, economically disadvantaged groups.
7. Past summer youth employment programs cited in the chapter resulted in:
    a. significant long-term employment creation for minority youth.
    b. significant short-term employment creation for minority youth.
    c. no significant employment creation for minority youth.
    d. negative long-term employment creation for minority youth.

Essay Questions

1. Summarize and explain the four key lessons learned from the social science research examined in the chapter.

2. Summarize and explain the main arguments and conclusions put forth by Anderson in the chapter.

3. Summarize and explain the main conclusions Anderson draws from his examination of social science research relating to the employment and training option.

4. Discuss the "pros" and "cons" of the federal government's continued support of employment and training programs designed to increase the earnings of economically disadvantaged groups. Draw on evidence from the readings and/or your own personal experiences and observations to support your essay.

Additional Essay Questions

5. Should the federal government invest more money into employment and training programs for the urban poor, even if such investments come at the expense of support for other strategies to increase the earnings of this specific target group? Explain, using specific evidence from Anderson's chapter or other selections in the book to support your argument.

6. According to Anderson, the Center for Employment and Training (CET) in San Jose, California is one of the most successful employment and training programs. To learn more about the program, visit CET's website, www.cetweb.org/index.html. Based on the information on CET's website, the readings, and your personal observations, what makes the CET program so successful? Why might it be difficult to replicate this successful program?

C H A P T E R

35

Racism in U.S. Welfare Policy: A Human Rights Issue

Linda Burnham

Key Terms and Institutions

1995 Beijing Platform for Action
Convention on the Elimination of
   All Forms of Discrimination
   Against Women
Family cap
Food insecurity
Food stamps
International Convention on Economic,
   Social, and Cultural Rights
Living wage
Minimum wage

Official poverty level
Personal Responsibility and Work
   Opportunity Reconciliation Act
   (PRWORA)
Social dynamic
Underclass
Underemployment
Universal Declaration of Human Rights
Welfare reform
Workfare

Note: The true/false and multiple-choice questions below are ranked according to level
of difficulty. For example, true/false questions # 1 and 2 below are less difficult
than questions # 9 and 10.

True/False Questions

Indicate whether each of the following statements is True or False by placing a "T" for true or an "F" for false in the space provided.

_____ 1. Once welfare recipients become ineligible for welfare benefits, they also lose access to government programs such as Medicare and food stamps.

_____ 2. Women of marginalized racial groups are disproportionately represented among current welfare recipients.

_____ 3. Due to the "family cap" policy, women who have children while receiving welfare benefits are not entitled to an adjustment in the amount of benefit received.

_____ 4. Although the unemployment rate decreased during the 1990s, the chapter concludes that high rates of unemployment for less-educated workers made it difficult for welfare recipients to find work.

_____ 5. Although some former welfare recipients' income increased when they found employment, the costs associated with working made their access to food less secure.

_____ 6. The author states that women of color comprise the majority of those receiving low wages and working in substandard conditions.

_____ 7. Citing the United States Conference of Mayors, 1999; the chapter states that homeless families increased to an estimated 37 percent of total family population in 1999.

_____ 8. Homelessness exacerbates differences between average black and white net wealth in the United States, because most families' appreciable assets are concentrated in the home.

_____ 9. The passage of the PRWORA resulted in a decrease in the number of low-wage workers employed.

_____ 10. Workers with hourly earnings of $6.61 are "just above" the poverty level because such jobs tend to be part-time, yielding lower annual earnings than full-time work.

_____ 11. The service, sales, and clerical sectors are described by the author as "gender ghettos" because female former welfare recipients tend to be underrepresented in these sectors.

_____ 12. Underemployment rates are always equal to or higher than unemployment rates because those classified as unemployed are also classified as underemployed.

Multiple-Choice Questions

Circle the letter that corresponds to the (one) best answer.

1. In an Illinois study, the population reporting the most difficulty with food insecurity was:

    a. former welfare recipients not participating in the labor force.

    b. former welfare recipients who were participating in the labor force.

    c. current welfare recipients not participating in the labor force.

    d. low-wage workers who had never received welfare benefits.

2. All of the following are cited by the author as examples of economic and political mechanisms that re-create racial disparities *except*:

    a. the Personal Responsibility and Work Opportunity Reconciliation Act.

    b. political manipulation of negative racial stereotypes.

    c. federally-sponsored loans for higher education.

    d. "cutbacks," or decreases, in federal funding for welfare programs.

3. Which of the following is an explanation for the decrease in the value of the minimum wage during the 1980s and 1990s?

    a. Increases in the minimum wage were not sufficient to offset the effects of inflation.

    b. Some workers, such as women of color, were not subject to the minimum wage.

    c. Widespread immigration of single mothers to the United States.

    d. Welfare recipients' noncompliance with work requirements.

4. All of the following groups are excluded from receiving welfare benefits *except*:

    a. individuals convicted of drug felonies.

    b. individuals who immigrated illegally to the United States.

    c. children born to unmarried parents.

    d. teenaged mothers who are not living with their parents.

5. Which of the following is cited by the author as an aspect of U.S. welfare policy that violates the Universal Declaration of Human Rights?

    a. Time limits on the receipt of welfare benefits.

    b. Benefit payments differ in size for similar households of different races.

    c. Welfare recipients in some states must provide evidence that they are looking for work.

    d. "Cutbacks," or decreases, in federal funding for welfare programs.

6. As cited from Uchitelle (1997), welfare-to-work programs had which of the following effects on wages for low-paid jobs during the mid- to late 1990s?

    a. Wages increased during this time period.

    b. Wages were unchanged during this time period.

    c. Wages decreased during this time period.

    d. Wages decreased before the passage of PRWORA and subsequently increased.

7. All of the following suggested reforms would cost the federal government more money to implement *except*:

    a. ending time limits on receipt of benefits.

    b. regarding education as a work activity.

    c. increasing funding for housing assistance and childcare subsidies.

    d. disaggregating data on the outcomes of welfare reform by race, ethnicity, and gender at the county, state, and federal levels.

Essay Questions

1. Identify and explain at least two of the negative consequences of time limits on welfare benefit receipt as described by the author.

2. What examples do the author cite to explain why former welfare recipients who obtain jobs have difficulty providing their families with an adequate supply of food?

3. List three of the recommendations of human rights organizations for TANF reform. List three of the recommendations of human rights organizations for reforms not directly pertaining to TANF.

4. Why might the "family cap" and the denial of welfare benefits to teenaged mothers not living with their parents be violations of the Universal Declaration of Human Rights?

Additional Essay Questions

5. What are arguments supporting and contradicting the hypothesis that welfare reform violates the International Convention on the Elimination of All Forms of Racial Discrimination?
6. Compare and contrast the "personal responsibility" explanation of poverty with the "structural social dynamic" explanation of poverty.

PART

Understanding
Black Reparations

THE CHAPTERS IN PART VIII explore critical aspects of the growing and controversial reparations movement. The principal thrust of this movement is to obtain compensation for oppression and other losses experienced by blacks during the era of slavery. Some advocates extend the period for which reparations are warranted to include the post-slavery Jim Crow period. These extended claims build on assessments that the forces set in motion during slavery have had continuing negative effects on the economic advancement of African Americans. There is also well-documented evidence of systematic discrimination and expropriation of black-owned property after slavery ended. Taken together, the chapters provide a context for understanding these issues, as well as barriers to obtaining reparations and strategies for using reparations successfully to alter the economic fortunes of blacks.

Robert Allen's chapter, "Past Due: The African American Quest for Reparations," presents an overview of efforts by blacks to obtain reparations, dating back to the mid-nineteenth century and including current initiatives. Allen locates the reparations movement in the United States as part of a global challenge to the political economy of capitalism. The current global struggle to end racial discrimination and exploitation is of special importance to blacks in the United States, in part, because of the continuing assaults on affirmative action programs. Richard America's chapter, "The Theory of Restitution," presents a general theory of restitution that addresses liabilities that dominant groups incur when they impose unjust economic arrangements on less powerful groups. He applies this theory to African Americans, highlighting exploitative, exclusionary, and discriminatory processes that have distorted economic relations between blacks and whites. He also discusses policy options for paying reparations. In their chapter, "The Economics of Reparations," William Darity Jr. and Dania Frank discuss precedents for reparations payments to blacks emerging from the experiences of Native Americans, Japanese Americans, and Jews. They highlight the ways in which economic reasoning can provide guidance in resolving several critical issues that must be resolved for the reparations movement to be successful, including possible forms that reparations payments might take, sources of funds to pay reparations, and the magnitude of reparations due to blacks.

4. Summarize and explain the details of the Conyers Bill (HR891).

5. Summarize and evaluate Robert Allen's analysis of the cost of being black.

Additional Essay Questions

6. Summarize and evaluate Manning Marable's position on capitalism and black under-development.

7. Discuss the impact of FHA historical racial policies.

4. Describe each of the restitution remedies proposed by the author.

5. What is a discrimination index and what impact does the author suggest it might have?

6. Do you agree with the author that exposing economic injustices, in and of itself, leads to a reduction in the injustices? Cite evidence from the reading to support your argument.

Additional Essay Questions

7. How might an economist measure "fair" wages and returns to investment during the antebellum era, taking note of the effects of a reduced labor force due to slavery?
8. Using ethical and legal precedents from your own experience, discuss the validity of the author's argument justifying reparative redistribution (found in paragraph 5).

African American Economic Development and Urban Revitalization Strategies

THE CHAPTERS IN PART IX present various economic development and revitalization strategies to address some of the issues and challenges that face African Americans at the dawn of the new millennium. Conservative urban economic development and revitalization models assume that the private business sector holds the key to inner-city economic development. The first three chapters of this section either explicitly or implicitly reject the conservative private business-centered development model, and instead adopt community economic development principles and holistic, collaborative, and community-building strategies. The last two chapters of this section avoid an elaborate discussion of the major urban economic development models and principles. These chapters provide a limited range of practical solutions to a few of the most severe economic challenges facing inner-city communities. Collectively, the chapters in this section provide a comprehensive approach to inner-city economic development that will assist scholars in the field, public policy makers, and community activists in formulating solutions to such inner-city problems as high rates of black and Hispanic unemployment, lack of access to credit and financing, gentrification and displacement, and racial disparities in wealth and income.

The first chapter by John Whitehead, David Landes, and Jessica Gordon Nembhard, "Inner-City Economic Development and Revitalization: A Community-Building Approach," focuses on revitalizing inner-city communities through equitable development strategies and a community-building approach. Their chapter emphasizes the importance of attracting debt and equity capital to support the development of minority businesses that are linked to the high growth sectors of the economy. Kalima Rose's chapter, "Combating Gentrification through Equitable Development," significantly extends the discussion of the importance of community economic development strategies. This selection shows how equitable development strategies in particular can be used to reverse gentrification and displacement trends that often come with community revitalization and regional development patterns. Shondrah Nash and Cedric Herring's essay, "The Black Church and Community Economic Development," discusses the historic and contemporary involvement of the black church in generating community economic development and empowerment. While their chapter gives a detailed account of the use of holistic and cooperative strategies in a broad range of successful black church-sponsored ventures and campaigns, the chapter's unique contribution is its discussion of the role of the black church in furthering African American social capital formation.

Thomas D. Boston's chapter, "Black Patronage of Black–Owned Businesses and Black Employment," proposes another alternative for increasing African American employment opportunities—the development of African American businesses. As discussed earlier in the book, nonminority firms primarily hire white workers, while African American-owned businesses hire a very large percentage of minority workers. Thus, Boston favors more targeted support of African American businesses—most notably, blacks increasing their patronage of African American businesses—as one important way to alleviate black unemployment. In the last chapter, "African American Athletes and Urban Revitalization: African American Athletes as a Funding Source for Inner-City Investments," John Whitehead and James B. Stewart continue the discussion of financing inner-city economic development by examining the potential role of African American athletes as a major funding source for new inner-city investments. Their chapter provides a detailed analysis of the earnings of African American athletes in major U.S. sports, showing that this group represents one of the potential pools of sizeable black capital available for inner-city investments. The essay also identifies specific industries with significant potential for investment ventures by black athletes and examples of successful inner-city investment activities by this group, including pilot ventures undertaken by Earvin "Magic" Johnson.

4. The chapter puts forth seven core principles of community economic development. Which of these principles do you think would be the most controversial to advocates of the private business-centered development model? Explain your reasoning.

5. Summarize and briefly describe the main strategies advanced in the chapter to increase available capital in America's inner cities.

Additional Essay Questions

6. Briefly discuss Landes, Nembhard, and Whitehead's views regarding cooperative economic strategies.
7. Compare and contrast Porter's views regarding community development banks (CDBs) with those of Landes, Nembhard, and Whitehead.
8. An important principle of community economic development (CED) is emphasizing "social needs over profits" in urban revitalization campaigns. Do you agree or disagree with this principle? Explain your answer.

CHAPTER

40

Combating Gentrification through Equitable Development

Kalima Rose

Key Terms and Institutions

ACORN
Below market rate (BMR)
Community development block grant
(CDBG)
Community development corporation
(CDC)
Community land trusts (CLTs)
Community Reinvestment Act
Development trends
Disinvestment
Displacement-Free Zone
Equitable Development Tool Kit
Exclusionary zoning practices
Fifth Avenue Committee (FAC)
Financing strategies
Gentrification
Gentrification indicators
HOME federal grants
Housing affordability

Housing trust funds
Inclusionary zoning policies
Infrastructure
Land use and land use control
Limited equity housing cooperatives
Los Angeles' Figueroa Corridor
Coalition for Economic Justice
Mixed-use development
PolicyLink
Portland's Interstate Alliance to End
Displacement
Proactive financing strategies
Region development patterns
Real estate transfer tax
Reinvestment
San Francisco Mission District
Anti-Displacement Coalition
U.S. Department of Housing and
Urban Development (HUD)

Key Name

Kalima Rose

Note: The true/false and multiple-choice questions below are ranked according to level of difficulty. For example, true/false questions # 1 and 2 below are less difficult than questions # 9 and 10.

True/False Questions

Indicate whether each of the following statements is True or False by placing a "T" for true or an "F" for false in the space provided.

_____   1. Low-income individuals and people of color benefit the most from the development trends described by the author.

_____   2. Affordable housing is increasing due to the extensive investment in the housing needs of Americans by governmental bodies.

_____   3. Housing trust funds typically target households that earn about 30 to 50 percent of the area mean income.

_____   4. The most successful equitable development projects combine different organizations, multiple strategies, and interrelated development tools to achieve the defined goals.

_____   5. A Displacement-Free Zone was set up by the Fifth Avenue Committee (FAC) as an aid for the developers and their investors.

_____   6. An unexpected benefit to the FAC's work is the decline in evictions of residents in existing buildings.

_____   7. Gentrification consists of development projects created to benefit the current residents and small businesses of a community or neighborhood.

_____   8. According to the author, if equitable development practices were applied in the Bay Area Metropolitan Region, people in the poorer neighborhoods of the region would benefit.

_____   9. The recession, following the boom of the nineties, has not reversed the displacement brought on by the economic boom.

_____   10. One positive contribution of gentrification to a town or city is the increased tax revenues brought about by the escalating value of real estate.

_____   11. Land development practices and local zoning exclusions make it easy for developers to avoid creating housing to benefit poor people and people of color.

_____   12. Local needs of residents are the most important principle driving community development strategies.

_____   13. The author believes the FAC's "Displacement Free-Zone" is an ineffective organizing tool to mobilize affected residents in the lower Park Slope district of Brooklyn.

_____   14. Historically, redevelopment strategies such as urban renewal of the 1950s and 1960s successfully avoided large-scale displacement by working with community activists and political leaders.

Multiple-Choice Questions

Circle the letter that corresponds to the (one) best answer.

1. When the author discusses various stages of gentrification she means:
   a. milestones in a development continuum that begins with rising land and housing costs, and ends with higher-income newcomers.
   b. nonprofit and for-profit redevelopment.
   c. displacement and evictions brought about by higher rents.
   d. increasing support for social services networks and facilities.

2. Displacement causes the loss of all of the following *except*:
   a. cultural amenities associated with the neighborhood before the development project began.
   b. the inability of residents to reside where they were raised.
   c. churches and other religious institutions serving the residents.
   d. growth of commercial interests in the area.

3. Housing trust funds, inclusionary zoning, community land trusts (CLTs), and organizing are some of the tools used to:
   a. counter adverse effects of community gentrification.
   b. maximize profits for developers.
   c. improve political power for those who possess it.
   d. eliminate Jim Crow era developments.

4. A prospective developer, desiring a successful gentrification project, would seek a community that has the following:
   a. a high proportion of renters and location near a body of water.
   b. ease of access to job centers and a high proportion of home owners.
   c. a high proportion of owner-occupied dwellings and low housing values.
   d. buildings of architectural merit with low values and location in a region of high congestion.

5. Strategies to counter gentrification's burdens on existing residents include:
   a. impose real estate transfer taxes to fund current residents' needs for affordable housing.
   b. assessment of community needs and development of plans to discriminate against white housing applicants.
   c. plan for existing residents' needs after the project is ratified by the local governing body or authority.
   d. none of the above.

6. Kalima Rose's four fronts require action to counter the effects of gentrification through:

a. stabilizing existing businesses by improving their bottom line through a "support local businesses" campaign.
b. controlling the land with land giveaways for the benefit of new business investments.
c. connecting land development strategies to regional opportunities that will explicitly benefit the poor and people of color in the community.
d. eliminating key resident services.

7. Kalima Rose describes various ways to stabilize existing renters. Which of the following group of strategies would most likely achieve this purpose?
a. Creating emergency funds, building parks, and wiring for high technology.
b. Removing discriminatory behaviors, repealing rent control, enforcing policies to evict existing tenants.
c. Enforcing "just cause" eviction protections, rent control, inclusionary zoning, and creating limited equity housing cooperatives.
d. Creating land swaps, emergency rental assistance funds, and tax write-offs to major corporation's businesses.

8. When Kalima Rose refers to "a Real Estate Transfer Tax that is indexed for speculation" she most likely means that:
a. this transfer tax rate will rise as home prices rise.
b. this tax will be higher if someone buys and sells often.
c. it is good to tax real estate because it is not a productive asset.
d. the tax will improve the liquidity of the housing market.

9. Assuming that the 14 million U.S. owner and renter households who spent more than half their income on housing in 1999 had an aggregate income of $210 billion, then they typically spent:
a. over $7500 per year on housing.
b. an indeterminate amount per year on housing because the percentage of income spent on housing grows as income grows.
c. far too much on fast food.
d. over $9700 per year on housing.

Essay Questions

1. Explain the cycle of gentrification.

2. What are the reasons a particular neighborhood is more susceptible to gentrification than another.

3. Describe the evolution of a community redevelopment process.

4. Describe why people of color and the poor are most adversely affected by gentrification.

5. Explain what is meant by equitable development.

6. Briefly list the four tools for equitable development and explain how the fourth action to preserve and expand affordable housing can underwrite the action on the first three.

Additional Essay Questions

7. Describe how the four development trends are detrimental to people of color and poor people living in proposed areas for gentrification.
8. One of the policies that is sometimes advocated to help make housing equitable is rent control. What problems might such a policy bring? Do you think such a policy is justified in terms of costs and benefits?

Extra Credit

Taking the model for equitable development as described by Kalima Rose, apply it to your own community or another community (if yours is inappropriate) and devise a strategy to counter the adverse affects of gentrification and community revitalization. Make this proposal four to six pages (or more if you are so inspired), 1.5 spaces between lines.

_____

N A M E

C H A P T E R

41

The Black Church and Community Economic Development

Shondrah Nash and Cedric Herring

Key Terms and Institutions

Allen A. M. E. Church
Allen Housing Development Fund
Beneficial societies
Bronx Christian Fellowship
Civil War
Community development corporations (CDCs)
Community economic development
Cooperative Enterprises
Faith-based initiatives
First African Methodist Episcopal Church
Grace Baptist Church Elmwood
Greater Centennial A. M. E. Zion
Great Depression
Knight and Daughters of Tabor

Nation of Islam
Opportunities Industrial Centers
Project Triumph
Protestant values
Quasi-religious mutual aid
Rainbow/Push Coalition
Social capital
Southern Christian Leadership Conference (SCLC)
United Presbyterian Church
White House Office of "Faith-Based" and Community Initiatives
Wheat Street Baptist Church
Wall Street Project

Key Names

Richard Allen
President George W. Bush
Reverend Moses Dickson
Rev. Jesse Jackson
Absalom Jones

Abraham Lincoln
Elijah Mohammed
Edwin Stanton
Leon Sullivan
Booker T. Washington

Note: The true/false and multiple-choice questions below are ranked according to level of difficulty. For example, true/false questions # 1 and 2 below are less difficult than questions # 9 and 10.

True/False Questions

Indicate whether each of the following statements is True or False by placing a "T" for true or an "F" for false in the space provided.

_____   1. Religion was the single most important source of early black involvement in economic development.

_____   2. The black church influence on federal policy toward freed slaves was significant in the period immediately following the Civil War.

_____   3. In the post–Civil War period, black self-help initiatives tended to promote Protestant values.

_____   4. According to Eric Lincoln, the Nation of Islam's self-help programs do not operate according to the behavioral rules followed by capitalist enterprises.

_____   5. Under Rev. Leon Sullivan's "10–36 plan," church congregates gave $10.00 for 36 months to a community-sponsored investment initiative.

_____   6. Relatively few white religious organizations participate in community development activities

_____   7. Lincoln and Mamiya's research suggests that few conservative congregations participate in community services.

_____   8. Nash and Herring's analysis suggests that the black church's effort to provide jobs skills and placement services has been successful.

_____   9. Home equity as a percentage of total wealth is greater for blacks than for other ethnic groups.

_____   10. In general, CDCs have been successful in meeting their objectives.

_____   11. Jesse Jackson's Wall Street Project is immediately concerned with increasing black economic and political power.

_____   12. Black church community development projects have tended to use holistic strategies.

_____   13. In recent years, the black church has become increasingly involved in promoting social capital networks among African Americans.

_____   14. Most of America's stock of social capital has been generated outside of religious institutions.

_____   15. Nash and Herring suggest that African Americans should place greater emphasis on developing collaboration between black and white institutions in order to advance black economic power and wealth.

Multiple-Choice Questions

Circle the letter that corresponds to the (one) best answer.

1. The early emergence of black quasi-public religious mutual aid and beneficial societies can be strongly linked to:
   a. direct financial support from white philanthropists.
   b. federal government-sponsored aid to address black economic disenfranchisement.
   c. the black community's need for economic cooperation.
   d. none of the above.

2. Which of the following is *least* important in explaining why black churches are in a relatively strong position to sponsor community economic development initiatives?
   a. The ability of black churches to build and sustain social capital networks.
   b. The ability of black churches to take advantage of economies of scale benefits.
   c. The experience black churches bring in managing employment development and placement programs.
   d. The ability of black congregations to raise large sums of money.

3. Nash and Herring's analysis implies that there is:
   a. a direct relationship between the size of government and support for black church's involvement in developing job skills and job placement activities.
   b. an inverse relationship between the size of government and support for black church's involvement in developing job skills and job placement activities.
   c. no clear relationship between the size of government and support for black church's involvement in developing job skills and job placement activities.
   d. broad support for the black church's involvement in developing job skills and job placement activities.

4. A major shortcoming of church-based CDCs relates to their:
   a. emphasis on developing church-sponsored economic development initiatives.
   b. commitment to building social capital networks.
   c. very broad mission statements.
   d. hiring practices.

5. "Social capital" refers to:
   a. the stock of public goods.
   b. a group's stock of human capital.
   c. a group's ability to cooperate with other groups.
   d. a group's friendship networks, intragroup cooperation, and collective identity.

6. Which of the following is *not* true of President Bush's "Faith-Based" initiatives?
   a. They are designed to bolster support for the privatization of "public goods."
   b. They are designed to win black church support for republican economic proposals.
   c. They are consistent with community economic development principles.
   d. They would lead to greater federal tax dollars going to black churches.

Essay Questions

1. Discuss the black church's role and activities in furthering black economic development in the post–Civil War period. Be sure to cite examples.

2. What was Booker T. Washington's philosophical approach to black economic advancement?

3. Explain why the black church is in a unique position to effectively sponsor community economic development activities.

4. Describe the black church's current employment services. For which type of jobs are these services designed?

5. Describe the activities and accomplishments at least two church-sponsored cooperative enterprises.

6. Describe what is meant by "social capital." Discuss the role and activities of U.S. religious institutions in building and sustaining social capital networks.

Additional Essay Question

7. What functions and services do community development corporations (CDCs) perform? What are the major problems associated with church-sponsored CDCs?

C H A P T E R

42

Black Patronage of Black-Owned Businesses and Black Employment

Thomas D. Boston

Key Terms and Institutions

Business census

Buying power

Disaggregate

Disposable income

EEO1 report

Industrial category

Joint Center for Political Economic
  Studies

Personal service establishment

Purchasing power

Retail establishment

Survey of Minority-Owned Business
  Enterprises (SMOBE)

U.S. Bureau of Labor Statistics

U.S. Department of Labor

Workforce/labor force

Key Names

Timothy Bates

Thomas Boston

Jeffery Humphreys

Note: The true/false and multiple-choice questions below are ranked according to level of difficulty. For example, true/false questions # 1 and 2 below are less difficult than questions # 9 and 10.

True/False Questions

Indicate whether each of the following statements is True or False by placing a "T" for true or an "F" for false in the space provided.

_____   1. Between 1992 and 1997, the number of black-owned businesses increased at a faster rate than the corresponding growth rate for *all* businesses.

_____   2. By 2010, black-owned businesses are projected to provide jobs for close to 10 percent of the black workforce.

_____   3. In 2002, 6.8 percent of employed black workers were employees of black-owned businesses.

_____   4. The chapter implies that we can look at changes in total employment in black-owned firms, by industry, to draw conclusions about changes in industry distribution of black-owned firms.

_____   5. There is an inverse relationship between black patronage of black-owned firms and black employment.

_____   6. The only industry to experience an absolute decline in the number of black-owned businesses was the mining industry.

_____   7. Using Thomas Boston's method of examining the changing industry distribution of black-owned businesses, it can be inferred that, from 1982–1997, the transportation, commodities, and utilities industry experienced the largest increase in its *share* of black-owned businesses.

_____   8. The question "How much total Black purchasing power is spent with Black-owned businesses?" refers to the percentage of blacks' disposable income spent at black-owned businesses.

_____   9. To estimate the projected employment of black workers by black-owned firms, the author uses an employment growth measure that takes into account the fact that the *percentage* of black employees hired by these firms will be increasing between now and 2010.

_____   10. According to the first paragraph of the chapter, employment in black-owned businesses increased by 9.8 percent between 1982 and 1997.

_____   11. Using Thomas Boston's method of examining the changing industry distribution of black-owned businesses, it can be inferred that, from 1982–1997, the services industry experienced the largest increase in the number of black-owned businesses.

_____   12. We can calculate the proportion of black total purchasing power spent with black-owned businesses by dividing the amount of revenue of black-owned businesses earned from blacks, by the sum of all black individuals' income.

_____   13. From the author's analysis of the Atlanta EEO1 reports, we can infer that the majority of all firms in Atlanta are owned by blacks.

Multiple-Choice Questions

Circle the letter that corresponds to the (one) best answer.

1. According to the chapter, there has been an increase in the number of black-owned businesses in the _____ industry.
   a. entertainment
   b. accounting
   c. construction contracting
   d. none of the above

2. All of the following were reasons for the change in the composition of black-owned businesses during the 1970s and 1980s *except*:
   a. the decline of racial segregation, continuing from the 1960s.
   b. the diminished influence of affirmative action.
   c. the increasing number of black individuals with business degrees.
   d. the greater accumulation of human capital in the black community.

3. The characteristic that the author uses to measure the "quality" of employment provided by black-owned businesses versus other businesses is:
   a. the likelihood of being employed in a professional service industry.
   b. the wage rate and income levels of black employees relative to the levels of other employees.
   c. the attractiveness and safety of health environment.
   d. none of the above.

4. Since 13.5 percent of all black employees of black-owned firms worked in engineering and management services, as opposed to 1.6 percent of black employees of white-owned firms, we can conclude that:
   a. a greater proportion of black-owned firms, versus white-owned firms, specialize in engineering and management services.
   b. white-owned firms discriminate against black employees.
   c. skilled black workers in Atlanta tend to choose black employers over white employers.
   d. the chapter doesn't provide enough information to choose.

5. Inferring from data in the chapter, _____ black individuals were employed by black-owned firms in 2003.
   a. 1,258,765
   b. 823,499
   c. 1,007,012
   d. 718,341

6. To determine that 8 out of 10 jobs in black-owned firms are held by black employees, the chapter:
   a. calculates the ratio of black employees to all employees in black-owned firms.
   b. asks black business owners how likely they are to hire black employees.
   c. uses Bureau of Labor Statistics data to compute the total number of black employees and the number of black employees of black-owned firms.
   d. doesn't provide enough information to choose between the above options.

Essay Questions

1. What evidence does the chapter provide to argue that black individuals should increase their patronage of black-owned businesses?

2. What characteristics determine the relative "quality" of employment in different firms? Cite examples from the chapter and from your own experience.

3. Discuss the connection between the accumulation of human capital by blacks during the latter decades of the twentieth century and the industrial composition of black-owned businesses.

4. How might an economist show (using data from the Bureau of Labor Statistics) that every $1 million in revenue to black-owned firms generates 8 new jobs for black workers?

Additional Essay Question

5. What is the potential effect, both on black workers employed by black-owned and by non-black-owned businesses, of a doubling of black individuals' spending at black-owned businesses? What is the net effect on levels of black employment?

CHAPTER

African American Athletes and Urban Revitalization: African American Athletes as a Funding Source for Inner-City Investments

John Whitehead and James B. Stewart

Key Terms and Institutions

Boston Bank of Commerce
Canyon-Johnson Urban Fund
Champion Ventures
Communitarian argument
Conspicuous consumption
Economies of scale
Emerging lines of minority business
Enterprises
Equity capital
Family Saving's Bank
Founder's Bank
Fund-of-funds
Group contact

Human capital
Information economy
Information imperfections
Institutional investors
Johnson Development Corporation
Limited partnerships
Major League Baseball (MLB)
National Basketball Association (NBA)
National Football League (NFL)
Private equity firms
Traditional lines of minority business
    enterprise

Key Names

Hank Aaron	Earvin "Magic" Johnson
Harry Edwards	Paul Robeson
Richard Edwards	James B. Stewart
Janet Jackson	Robert E. Weems

Note: The true/false and multiple-choice questions below are ranked according to level of difficulty. For example, true/false questions # 1 and 2 below are less difficult than questions # 9 and 10.

True/False Questions

Indicate whether each of the following statements is True or False by placing a "T" for true or an "F" for false in the space provided.

_____   1. Table 43.1 shows that black NFL players have a higher average annual salary than black NBA players.

_____   2. According to Table 43.1, the combined annual salaries of black athletes in the three major sports was about $2.6 billion.

_____   3. There is less inequality in earnings among black athletes *across* the three major sports than *within* each major sport.

_____   4. In Table 43.2, the total number of black athletes within each major sport is first ranked by earnings and then split into five groups of equal size.

_____   5. James B. Stewart's communitarian argument suggests that athletes do not have an obligation to support community economic development initiatives.

_____   6. Michael Porter's research shows that most inner cities are near clusters of companies that are in the same industry and region.

_____   7. Stewart and Whitehead believe that business ventures undertaken by Earvin "Magic" Johnson can serve as a model for how black athletes can participate in urban revitalization.

_____   8. In most inner cities, there are a variety of unrecognized and untapped competitive advantages and opportunities to build highly profitable businesses.

_____   9. Imperfect information about the inner city has very little bearing on the lack of inner-city investments by black athletes.

_____   10. Reducing the extent of earnings inequality among black professional athletes would likely increase their involvement in inner-city investment initiatives.

_____   11. "Traditional black firms" tend to focus on serving black consumers, while "emerging black firms" tend to focus on serving a racially diverse clientele.

_____   12. Stewart and Whitehead's analysis suggests that economic self-interest arguments should be part of efforts to increase black athlete participation in inner-city investment initiatives.

_____   13. The propensity of black athletes to invest in the inner city is strongly influenced by communitarian considerations.

_____ 14. Champion Ventures is a "fund-of-funds" focused on minority markets.

_____ 15. Targeted "fund-of-funds" can reduce risk by diversifying their investments.

_____ 16. Minority-focused private equity firms are a major source of equity capital for black firms operating in the emerging lines of minority enterprise.

_____ 17. International specialization in producing athletes in certain sports tends to support Stewart's communitarian argument.

_____ 18. Champion Ventures represents a private equity "fund-of-funds" managed by former professional athletes.

_____ 19. Minority-focused private equity firms receive most of their capital from institutional investors.

_____ 20. A major criticism of Stewart's communitarian argument is that efforts to require athletes to contribute a percentage of their earnings to community economic development initiatives would lead to resource misallocation.

_____ 21. Some of the business ventures undertaken by Johnson Development Corporation fall within the so-called emerging fields.

_____ 22. Rick Edward's "group contract" idea tends to contradict Stewart's communitarian argument.

_____ 23. Stewart and Whitehead's analysis contradicts the idea that the special attention black high school athletes now receive in the public school system leads to socially inefficient outcomes.

Multiple-Choice Questions

Circle the letter that corresponds to the (one) best answer.

1. Following Whitehead and Stewart's analysis, all of the below statements are true _except_:
   a. High earning black athletes constitute one of the potential pools of sizable black capital available for inner-city investments.
   b. Pilot ventures undertaken by Earvin "Magic" Johnson represent an anomaly and cannot be used as models for a broad-based inner-city investment movement spearheaded by black athletes.
   c. It is generally easier to amass investment capital from one or a few wealthy individuals who can be persuaded about a particular investment than from many less wealthy individuals.
   d. All of the above statements are _true_.
2. Black NFL players in the lowest quintile in table 43.2 earned about what proportion of total earning among black athletes in the NFL?
   a. 1 percent.
   b. 4 percent.
   c. 7 percent.
   d. 11 percent.

3. Black NBA players in the middle quintile in table 43.2 earned about what proportion of total earning among black athletes in the NBA?
   a. 3 percent.
   b. 7 percent.
   c. 13 percent.
   d. 24 percent.
4. Which of the following statements is *not* true?
   a. The earnings gap among black athletes in MLB is wider than the earnings gap for black athletes in the NFL.
   b. The earnings gap among black athletes in the NBA is less pronounced than the earnings gap for black athletes in the MLB.
   c. The average salary for black NBA players in the highest quintile in table 43.2 is higher than the average salary for highest quintile black MLB players.
   d. All of the above statements are true.
5. Legally speaking, most of Earvin "Magic" Johnson's business ventures are:
   a. corporations.
   b. partnerships.
   c. sole proprietorships.
   d. none of the above.
6. Following Robert Weems's analysis, one large black insurance company would:
   a. bring the advantages of economies of scale to the black insurance industry.
   b. lead to a higher per unit cost for the black insurance industry than presently exists.
   c. in the long run, result in a smaller demand for black insurance industry products and services.
   d. none of the above.
7. Stewart and Whitehead's analysis suggests that more equality in earnings among black professional athletes would likely lead to:
   a. more inner-city investments by this group.
   b. less inner-city investments by this group.
   c. no change in the volume of inner-city investments by this group.
   d. a major increase in black athletic performance.
8. Which of the following negates the argument that black athletes have a historical-moral duty to support urban revitalization?
   a. Conservative/free market arguments that emphasize the individualistic nature of athletic performance.
   b. The progressive nature of the U.S. tax system.
   c. Specialization in producing athletes in certain sports that has occurred on a global scale.
   d. A and b above.
9. Which of the following supports Stewart's communitarian argument?
   a. The idea that efforts to equalize earnings among athletes would lead to social inefficiency.
   b. The current distribution of earnings among black athletes in the three major sports.
   c. Current tax policies.
   d. The international specialization of sports.

10. Conservative/free market economists would likely argue that:
    a. black athletes have a formal obligation to support community economic development initiatives.
    b. efforts to reduce earnings inequality among athletes will lead to resource misallocation.
    c. Stewart's communitarian argument lacks support of statistical evidence.
    d. none of the above.

11. The most effective way for black athletes to support urban revitalization is through:
    a. channeling their capital into private equity funds focused on minority markets.
    b. giving large donations to church-sponsored inner-city economic development initiatives.
    c. joining marketing campaigns to increase black patronage of the black insurance industry and other black financial institutions.
    d. none of the above.

12. Which of the following is *not* true?
    a. Targeted "fund-of-funds" help to serve the capital needs of other more specialized private equity funds.
    b. Interest in targeted "fund-of-funds" has increased in recent years as a result of the reemergence of individual investors as a source of equity capital.
    c. Targeted "fund-of-funds" are typically backed by private equity funds.
    d. Targeted "fund-of-funds" are typically structured as limited partnerships.

Essay Questions

1. Summarize and explain James Stewart's communitarian argument.

2. Give three major criticisms of Stewart's communitarian argument.

3. Describe and explain the economic self-interest argument for broader black athlete participation in community economic development initiatives.

4. Summarize the competitive advantages of the inner city identified by Michael Porter.

5. Give at least two reasons why black athletes have not invested in America's inner cities.

6. What is the best way that black athletes can support inner-city development according to Stewart and Whitehead?

Additional Essay Questions

7. Describe and explain the major weaknesses of the conservative/free market position that an athlete's income reflects his or her individual investments.
8. Describe the main features of "fund-of-funds."
9. Describe the main characteristics of Champion Ventures. Then discuss the limits of Champion Venture as a model for economic development initiatives involving black athletes.
10. Describe two examples of successful inner-city investment activities led by black athletes.
11. Describe and explain how black athletes can help save and strengthen black-owned financial institutions.